Anne Liberty

Paper Quilling

for Beginners
and Projects

A Simple Guide to Learn the Chinese Art of
Paper Quilling.

Basics, Techniques and Projects

Table of Contents

Introduction

Paper quilling is the craft of rolling strips of paper and gluing them to the surface to create an intricate three-dimensional piece of artwork. With the help of a quilling tool, you can coil strips into shapes; when the paper is rolled around a quill, the shapes are arranged to create beautiful art pieces.

They can be glued and shaped to form decorative art designs like jewelry, cards, flowers, picture frames, etc. The craft is becoming an extremely popular hobby among paper craftsmen, even though it is by no means a new form of art, the popularity is quite impressive, the increase in popularity is also an attribute of the fact that the art can be easily learned by children and adults, as long as you have a creative spirit, the paper quilling will be so interesting and enjoyable to you.

Unlike other papercraft, quilling is the easiest way to learn; it only takes mastery of basic techniques and be sure to create uniform sizes, with this in mind, it is possible to be an expert in no time. Paper quilling is a very simple decorative artwork that even a novice can master in an hour or two; although your imagination can only limit the possibilities, the decorative pieces can be the same.

Moreover, the cost of craft is almost nothing, so if you're looking to start it as a leisure activity or a source of income, paper quilling is one of the most important craft work you can do without stress or have a second thought of investing in, because decorative art designs can pay more than you've invested in.

Fundamental Quilling Technique

First and foremost, be creative because creativity matters a lot; you need to understand the basics and be more focused on the practice often for a while before you can roll or roll perfectly. Also try to make coils with different shapes and colors; when you've managed to make enough coils, all you need is to arrange them bit by bit on a sheet of drawing paper to form a pattern or a pattern.

And suppose they turn out to be good enough, and you're happy with the pattern. In that case, you might even want to show it to your family and friends to see, but before you show it off, make sure you put a little bit of glue on the coils to make it stick to the drawing paper. Then let the glue dry up before you display your quilled designs. Using this method, you'll come up with great designs.

There's a way you can roll a coil around a needle tool. First, you have to put the end on the index finger of one hand while holding the tool in the other.

Use your thumb and index finger to roll the paper strips around the needle tool while holding it firmly; it only takes rolling the paper to the end of your strips to get a coil, that's it, it's just so easy and fun to take a look at the picture below.

You may feel nervous at first, but once you master how to set your thumb and index finger to roll the paper strips around the needle tool, then you're good to go, you'll come up with different shapes.

At your spare time, take your time to practice paper quilling; you'll be so surprised to come up with beautiful quilling shapes and sizes even better than those in the photos, happy quilling.

What is Quilling?

Paper quilling is the craft of taking long, slender pieces of paper and curling, bending, and fringing them into shapes that are utilized in making paper arts and card making. Besides being one of the most alleviating papercraft strategies out there, quilling is a massive flexible technique. It has enjoyed a sudden comeback from the last decade, with paper artistry and quilled designs showing up on banners, high roads, and prominent advertising campaigns.

During the Renaissance, nuns and priests moved gold-overlaid paper leftovers during the bookmaking cycle and used them to animate strict articles as an option in contrast to exorbitant gold filigree. Quilling later turned into a diversion of eighteenth and nineteenth-century youngsters in England, who might finish service trays and household items with paper filigree. The training crossed the Atlantic with pioneers, who added quilling to light sconces and plate as home enhancements or decorations.

In the entirety of that time, the cycle has stayed the equivalent particularly; however, quilling plans and claim to fame supplies have unquestionably gotten up to speed to the 21st century. Today a few fans center around making unfathomably point by point 3-D figures, while others favor divider measured gallery establishments. Maybe quilling is most popular, however, as a method of carrying character to high-quality cards.

The short rundown of necessities incorporates portions of lightweight paper, stick, and an apparatus with which to roll the paper — that is it! Far and away superior, there's likely no compelling reason to search for provisions before you have a go at quilling, as a bamboo stick, round toothpick, or even a cake analyzer from your kitchen cabinet can fill in as a substitute device. Cut your own training takes from a sheet of normal PC paper, utilizing a paper shaper.

Numerous expressions and artworks stores sell essential devices and bundles of multicolor paper strips. Wonderful papers and other quilling supplies are accessible from online providers. Gracious, and ultimately, one prerequisite that is not accessible for procurement, yet will likewise be required, is a considerable measure of tolerance. With a little practice, in any case, I can nearly anticipate you'll discover quilling to be imaginatively fulfilling and fun.

Before you start quilling, here is all that you have to think about quilling. Quilling or paper filigree is a work of art that includes the utilization of portions of paper that are rolled, molded, and stuck together to make ornamental plans.

With the assistance of quilling, you can make keyrings, gems, enlivening things, Greeting cards, 3D models, and substantially more things. In this book, you can figure out how to begin with quilling, making essential shapes, making keyrings, ornamental things, bloom, and furthermore, some fundamental information about quilling. I likewise included loads of photographs for simple comprehension.

The History of Paper Quilling

Like many craft forms, paper quilling can trace its origins back hundreds of years to at least the 15th century (maybe earlier). It is believed to have been created by French and Italian nuns and used to decorate religious objects in an effort to save money. The lattice was fashioned to simulate carved ivory and wrought iron—two very costly details. When the paper quilling was gilded, it was hard to distinguish from metal, making it a good option for struggling churches.

Paper quilling had its heyday in England during the 18th century. In addition to embroidery, was considered a "proper pastime" for young women and was taught in boarding schools, as well as to "ladies of leisure" because it was seen as not too "taxing" for them. Quilling's influence spread to the United States, but the practice waned by the 19th century; there are relatively few examples of paper quilling during this time.

Tools To Prepare a Decorative Paper Quilling

When it comes to paper quilling, getting started might seem intimidating, but it's pretty simple — mainly because you only need a few supplies to master the basics. A quilling tool, some paper, and a dab of glue are all you need to begin learning this fun papercraft.

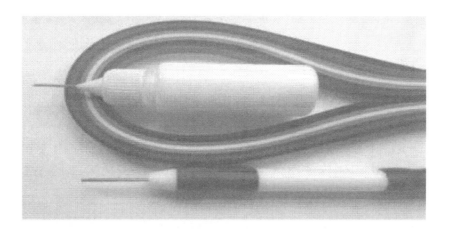

Working with those three tools, you'll get the basic quilling shapes down reasonably quickly. Soon after, you will inevitably want to put your new skills to use and make something extraordinary,

which means you'll add a few extra tools to your supply kit. Let's explore all of the new (and classic) paper quilling tools that are now available and the basics of how to use them.

Slotted Quilling Tool

The most common and easiest tool to learn with is the slotted quilling tool. By placing a quilling strip into the slot, you can easily and quickly roll the tool and create a coil to be

Shaped without the strip moving around much. The slot does leave a slight crimp in the centre of each spiral, which may not be to your liking. If that is the case, you can opt to use the next tool on our list.

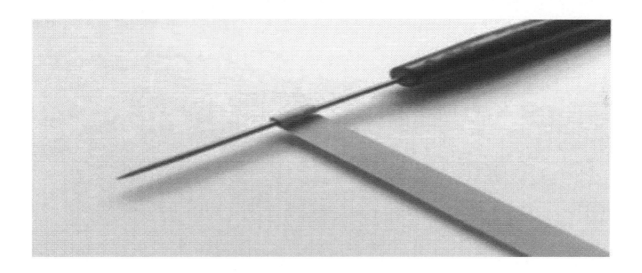

Needle Tool

When using a needle tool, you curl the paper around the needle and into a coil. The premise is simple enough, but it takes a bit of practice to become proficient and even longer to create coils quickly. Once you get the hang of it, however, you will be rewarded with extremely tiny and crimp-free centers.

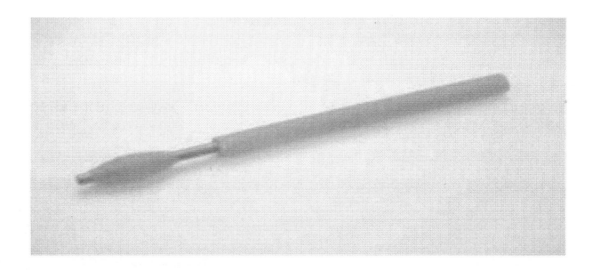

Paper Bead Tools

Paper bead tools are also extremely useful and can be used to create a variety of shapes

It is determined by how the paper has been cut. Similar in appearance and function to the slotted Quilling tool, the bead tool accommodates wider cuts and multiple strips of paper at once.

Quilling Paper

Of course, the paper is the most important material when it comes to quilling, but it's often also the most overlooked. A high-quality paper can make a huge contribution to the overall look of any quilling project.

Today's quilling paper suppliers offer a vast array of pre-cut quilling strips in numerous colors, widths, weights, and finishes. However, if you cannot find exactly what you need, you can easily cut your own with a ruler, self-healing mat, and a utility knife.

Quilling Forms

In recent years, a new wave of paper quilling tools has come to the surface, to the delight of quilling enthusiasts. Quilling forms have transformed the craft into many fun and exciting

Ways and they enable quillers to design and roll more freeform projects.

Stacked Forms

Stacked quilling forms let you create paper rings in many sizes without the need to purchase and store numerous dowel forms. These are often used to create an outside shape to fill in later. You can easily quill your own stacked quilling form using ½" quilling paper and a bead roller, or you can purchase one from a quilling paper retailer.

Needle Forms

Another useful addition to the quilling world: needle forms. These bamboo forms, originally

Used for knitting, allow quillers to create small rings of many sizes.

Scissors

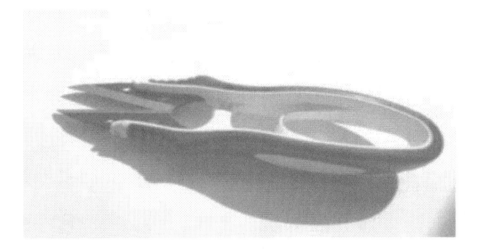

Good scissors are a must when quilling. Thread snipers, originally intended for sewing projects, work extremely well for the tiny paper cuts quilling calls for.

Quilling Glue

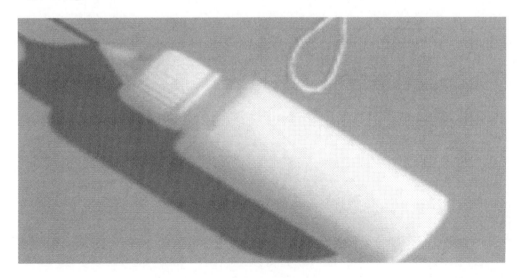

Last but not least on our must-have list is quilling glue in a needle-tip bottle. Using the suitable glue is just as important as using the right paper and tools, though which glue is best depends on personal preference. Glue can genuinely make or break your quilling experience and projects, so when trying out different types, keep in mind the ease of use and drying time.

Extra Quilling Materials

Cookie Cutters

Commonly used as a form in quilling (even though it was not intended for this purpose) is the cookie cutter. Quilling paper strips can be guided around and pretty much any shape, and a cookie-cutter helps contain strips in a predefined area.

This ornament made in the Shape of Michigan is an excellent example.

Quilling Molds

Quilling molds are used mostly in 3-D quilling, but the domes that are made from them can also be found in art. After creating a tightly closed coil with your quilling tool, you gently place it over the appropriately sized mold and glide the paper downward. Once the dome has been made, you can continue shaping it or apply glue on the inside surface to ensure it keeps its shape.

Fringing Scissors

Fringing scissors (in addition to regular scissors) are very useful when creating fringed flowers. The five blades create small strips that you can wind or quill to create flowers. A quilling fringier or a regular pair of scissors can also accomplish this style.

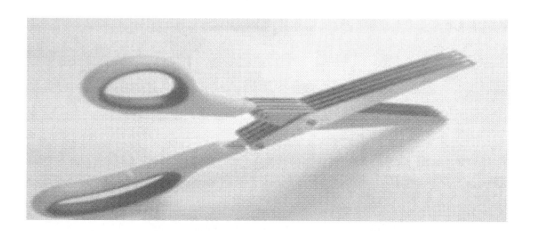

Quilling Comb

A quilling comb is a specialty tool that is used to create intricately laced loops. Individual or multiple strips can be weaved into infinite patterns and are often incorporated into floral art and landscapes.

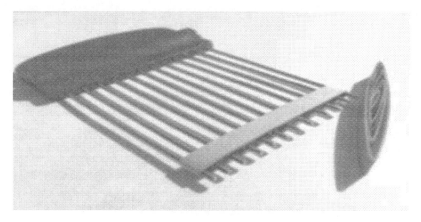

Quilling Guides

Quilling guides can be a huge help when first learning how to control your tool and paper (and for children who want to try the craft). Simply slide your slotted quilling tool in the guide before inserting paper, and you are ready to roll. The flat surface will ensure your coil stays put without springing open unexpectedly.

Tweezers

Angled tweezers are a must-have in any quiller's kit. When gluing or placing small pieces in place, these tweezers can be the only way to get the job done while keeping your sanity intact.

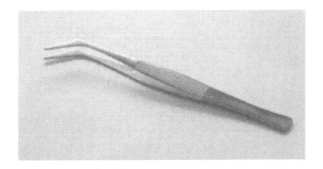

Circle Sizers

Circle sizers are great for beginning quillers to make uniform shapes. Recessed spaces allow you to release your coil without fear that it will be too loose or a different size from others. This version has a handy ruler, but other larger versions might have extra openings for projects that require exact symmetry.

Paper Quilling Tips for Beginners

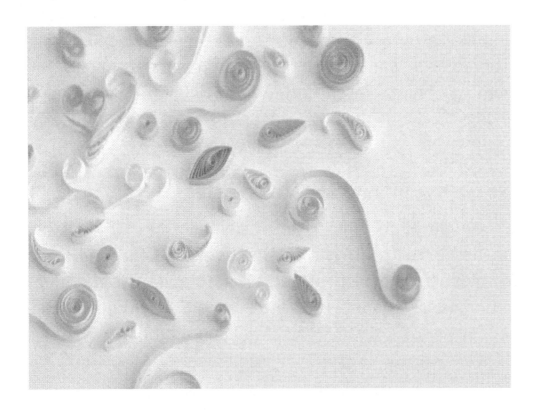

The art of Paper quilling is exciting. However, if you are a beginner, the learning curve process can be difficult and complex to learn. But not to worry, we have the perfect paper quilling tips to help beginners and make you become a pro.

1. Always Make Use of Colorful Backgrounds

A plain white background can be disturbing, while a colored background that provides lower contrast to your quilled shapes is more acceptable. It will help the viewers view how much you need them to look into and your decoration's general exquisiteness.

2. Select Thread Snippers Over Scissors

Selecting the right paper quilling tools is vital, and many scissors are not needed in this craft. Instead, you need a lightweight pair of thread snippers. They are the best for snipping off the glue-bound ends of quilling paper. Their little size aids them to fit easily and without any issue into any type of quilling toolbox.

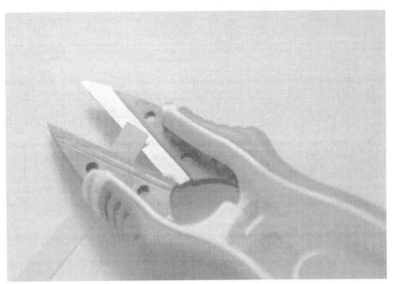

3. Obtain a Perfect Center in Every Coil

A needle tool is not needed to make perfect coils. Instead, you need a slotted tool that will provide you with the round center you crave for, and there would not be crimping if used the correct way.

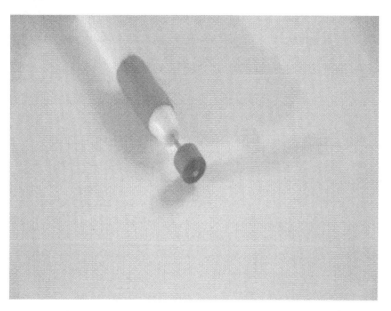

One major tip is to continue turning your quilling tool after getting to the end of your strip until you are satisfied that the tool does not stand in your way. The tool cuts the small piece of paper that would have resulted in the crimp, and then you would have the best coil. Meanwhile, if your quilling tool can't twist that way, there are other options that you can try out, like making use of a piercing tool or pin to smooth out the crimp.

4. Rip Instead of Snipping

There is no doubt that you want to produce clean lines and keep out all the seams in your shapes whenever you want it done. However, in some cases, there is no possible way to hide. If you are not impressed with how the sharp paper seams look like, you have the option of ripping the end of your quilling strip instead of an option to snip with scissors. When you do this, you will attachment will have a softer effect than a hard effect.

5. Roll With, Not Against, the Edge of the Quilling Strip

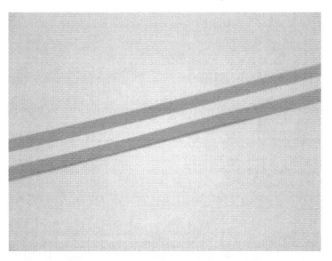

Whenever the quilling paper tears, the blade cuts it from an upward direction in a downward motion. The result of this is that the two long edges roll slightly downward. The effect is small and not noticeable, and that is why it isn't easy to see with your eye. However, it is possible to feel it when you run the strip among your fingers.

To get a perfect coil, you should roll with the curve, while the downward curve should face downwards. It may be quite tough to carry this out on your first few attempts, and omitting this step will not affect the looks of your quilling. However, whenever you begin to pay attention, performing it this way will become almost natural.

6. Use a Needle Form Before a Quilling Comb

Quilling comb can be quite difficult and uses a lot of time. You might begin to feel that they do not worth your time and effort but attempt this tip before you decide not to try it again.

First of all, roll a small coil with a quilling needle form, send the coil to your quilling comb, and produce your shape. This technique is that needle will form initially, before the quilling comb, and it would help keep the center of your coil where it should be.

7. Double Up Your Strips for a Grippy Roll

If you are rolling an additional large coil, the center will always end up breaking free from the quilling tool before you complete the process. The best you can attempt doing at that point is to roll the rest of it manually, which means by your hand. Meanwhile, you can prevent all that if you double up the strip to begin your coil.

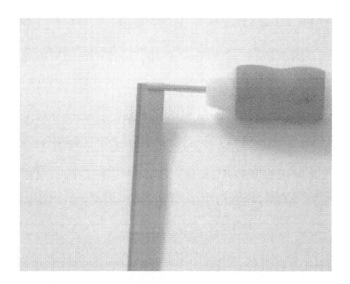

The double thickness will keep everything where it should be. To complete this process, there are two ways to try it out, one is by folding your first strip over, and the second is by using two strips on top of each other.

8. Use Nippers to Fix Your Mistakes

There is no one without a mistake in them, and no matter how you seem to be perfect in your work, nearly all project is likely to have a little issue somewhere. This is where the cuticle nippers are needed. You can get them in any drugstore in the nail care aisle.

Nippers will allow you to snip off a rough edge or take away unnecessary glue after it has dried.

9. Get Your Sponge Ready

A sponge is the right-hand man of a quiller, and an arrangement like the one you are seeing is delightful. The container does hold your needle-tip glue bottle upside down, which makes it ready to be used another time it is needed, while the moist sponge does not allow your glue from drying and congesting the tip. The surface of the sponge can be used to clean any glue that enters your fingers.

10. Be Friends With Your Eye Pin

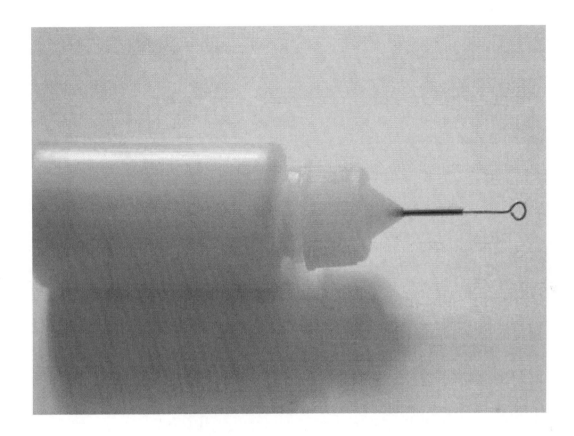

You left your cap off, and you can see that your needle tip is congested. It is not a problem; perhaps, you did not know about our sponge trick; check above for tip 9. But you still have a chance to change it. While using an eye pin, you can proceed to unplug the tip and move back to producing your art. The eye pin's blunt end makes it secure than a sewing pin. Do not leave the eye pin in the tip for an extended period since the pin is likely to rust and change your glue color.

Paper quilling has been popular since the 15th century, and there has been high demand in recent years. You can find paper quilling in cardmaking, paper flowers, and so on. It is amazing how you can produce complicated patterns and shapes from easy paper strips and glue.

Additional Paper Quilling tips for beginners

1. Make Use of Pre-cut Paper Strips for Your First Projects

Pre-cut paper quilling strips should be used for your first projects. Your first tries will have good outcomes if you use accurate machine-cut papers. When you relax with basic paper quilling methods, you can cut your paper strips and discover your creativity by trying out higher techniques.

2. Begin With Small Paper Quilling Projects

Begin with smaller sized projects initially. You can rapidly become weighed down if you attempt to solve a craft project that is too difficult for you. Smaller projects can encourage feelings of accomplishment, and it can be a ground on which to start to assist you to know your skills little by little. When you have known the basics, you can then proceed to try difficult projects with effortlessness.

3. Make Use of the Right Paper Quilling Tools

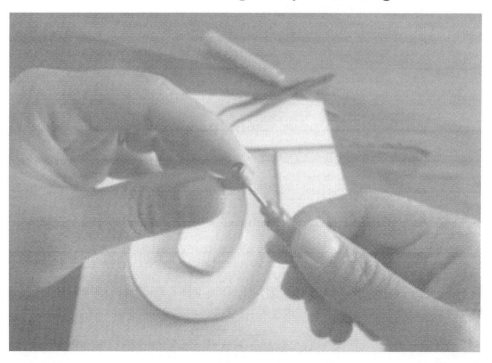

It is vital to select your quilling tools after long thinking. It is unnecessary to purchase any costly tools to form paper filigree art at first; a bamboo skewer or a toothpick will roll paper strips well. You can also buy a slotted quilling tool as well as a needle tool.

You can decide to place the strip of paper into the slotted tool's upper slot, which will provide you with high control when you are rolling the paper strips. If you do not know, a needle device is a sizeable tapered needle which handles is made of long wood. It assists you to hold it firmly when rolling strips of paper into different shapes. The two tools are of help when you are working on a difficult paper quilling projects.

4. Have a Light Tough When Using Glue with Paper Quilling

Whenever you are gluing your rolled paper shapes, do not forget to make use of glue cautiously. Using a lot of glue can rapidly spoil your project, which you might have worked on for a long time. You can prevent starting a project afresh with a little caution and carefulness. If it is not enough, you can always add more glue, but it is not possible to take away excess glue. Do not forget the design rule which states the Less is More.

5. Paper Quilling Patterns

Few beginners see using a premade quilling pattern as helpful when they begin. There are a lot of papers quilling patterns to buy or free download on the internet. The patterns found on the internet can assist beginners and aid them in building their skills.

What you are required to do is to place the printed pattern under a sheet of waxed paper and adhere to the instructions.

6. Master the Basic Paper Quilling Shapes

Understand the basic shapes before proceeding to work on a paper quilling project. It is very helpful to make a master page of basic paper quilling shapes. You can glue diverse shapes to a cardboard piece to use as a reference sheet when working on different projects.

7. Paper Quilling Circle Sizing Board

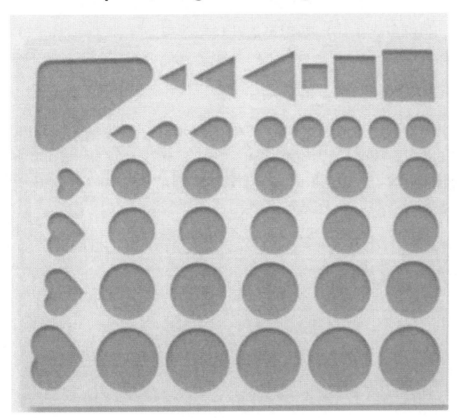

A circle sizing board is known as a tool that will surely be of help to you. The circle sizing board is a sheet of plastic that contains predrilled holes of different sizes and shapes. The holes assist you in rolling the paper quilling shapes.

The circle sizing board will also assist you to have stability in your paper quilling shapes.

8. Acetate Sheet

Develop your paper quilling rolled shape on top of a sheet of acetate. The acetate sheet is strong enough to provide your glued quilled shapes consistently. When the glue dries, you can then pull your quilled piece up off the sheet without harm. Simply wash the remaining glue from the acetate sheet and use it once again for your next project.

9. Join it With Other Craft

It is important to get more adventurous and use your quilled shapes in a mixture with other paper crafts to produce a more exciting design piece. Your quilled shapes can be combined to add more flare to:

- Decorative paper buckets

- Wall decorations and paintings

- Manually made jewelry boxes

10. Always Practice

There is no other option that can be substituted for practicing. Quilling, like other arts, needs a lot of practice to master the skill. If you want to be a pro and guru in quilling, you will have to be able to practice often, probably every day. Also, attempt to do more difficult shapes as you go along.

Paper Quilling Basics

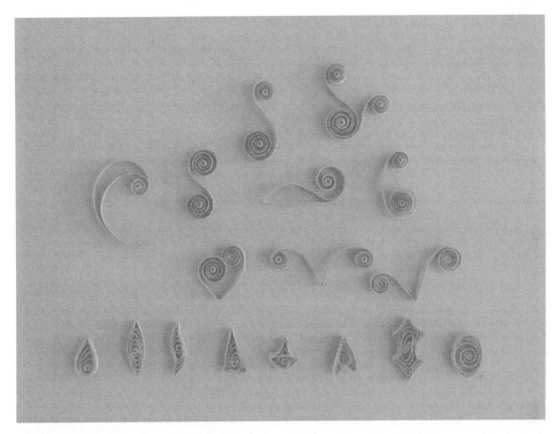

This guide's tasks highlight the tear loop, yet there are numerous other fascinating shapes to attempt — marquises, sharpened stones, holly leaves, and a wide range of lovely parchments, just to give some examples.

Supplies Needed:

Quilling paper: 1/8", standard width

Quilling device needle apparatus or opened instrument

Ruler

Scissors

Tweezers

Glue clear-drying, reasonable for paper

Plastic top to use as a glue palette

T-pin, paper penetrating apparatus, or round toothpick

Glass-head straight pins

Non-stick work board, stopper, or styrofoam something into which you can stick pins

Damp material to keep fingers liberated from stick

Procedures:

When buying an instrument, there are two essential sorts: an opened device and a needle device. The opened device is simplest to utilize; its lone burden is that space leaves a small crease in the loop's focal point. On the off chance that this is troublesome, buy a super fine opened device or attempt a needle instrument. The needle instrument is harder to ace, yet the prize will be a loop with a totally round focus.

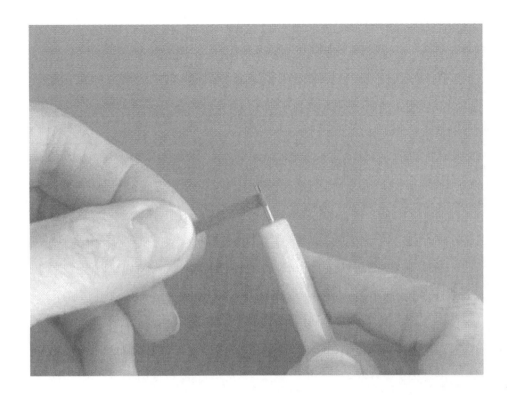

To roll a curl with an opened apparatus: Slide the finish of a strip into space, and turn the device with one hand while uniformly managing the strip with the other.

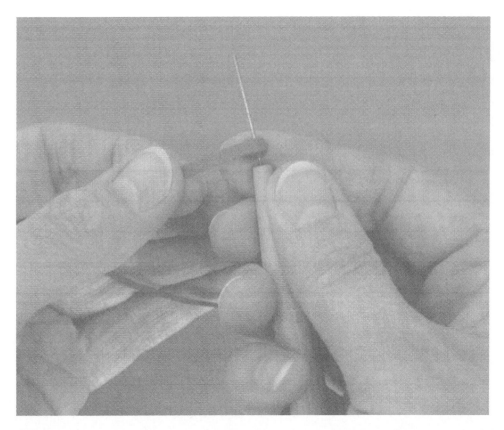

To roll a loop with a needle device: Dampen fingers and bend one finish of a strip over the needle. Roll the strip around the needle with the thumb and pointer of whichever hand feels generally great, applying even, firm weight, while holding the handle of the device with the other hand. Make certain to roll the paper, not the apparatus.

In utilizing an opened instrument or needle apparatus, when the strip is completely rolled, permit the loop to unwind, slide it off the device, and glue the end. Utilize just an exceptionally modest quantity of glue, applying it with the tip of a T-pin, penetrating paper apparatus, or toothpick. Hold the end set up for a couple of seconds while the glue dries. This is known as a free curl, and it's the fundamental shape from which numerous different shapes are made.

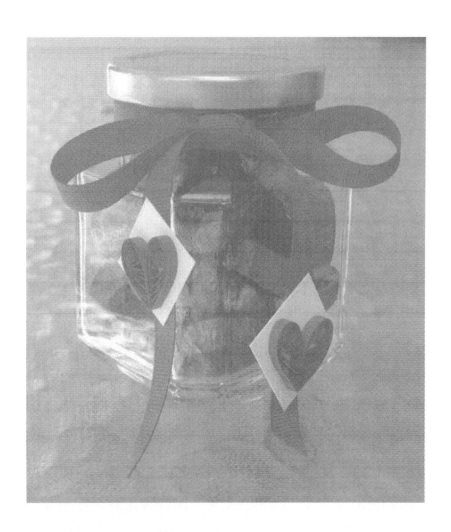

CANDY JAR PROJECT

Materials Needed:

Glass container

Grosgrain lace – red, 3/8"

Quilling paper, red, 1/8"

Cardstock, white

Cement froth dabs

Procedures

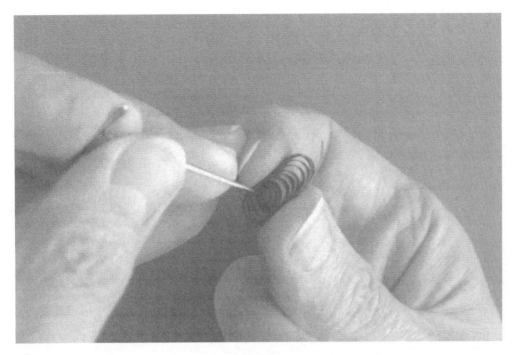

Stage 1: Make four tears. Roll a 12" free curl. Hold down the curl somewhat between your fingers; basically, you can utilize a pin to organize the inward loops so they are equally dispersed.

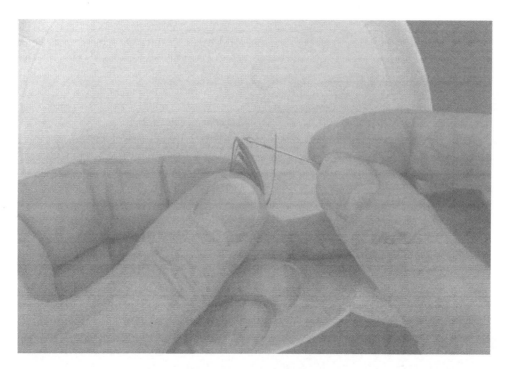

Squeeze strongly at the tip to come to a meaningful conclusion. Glue the end and trim the surplus paper.

Stage 2: Make two hearts. Spot 2 tears next to each other on the work board to make a heart shape, situating them in inverse headings so the inward loops seem to meet. Apply stick at the join spot.

Hold the tears set up with pins while the glue dries.

Stage 3: Fill a container with your preferred treat and tie a lace around it.

Stage 4: Cut two white, 1" cardstock squares and glue a heart on each.

Tip: When sticking a quilled object on a background, spread a shallow puddle of glue on a plastic holder cover or a sheet of waxed paper. Hold the quilling with tweezers and plunge its underside tenderly in a stick. Spot legitimately on the background.

Stage 5: Attach 1 square to every strip tail with a glue spot.

VALENTINE CARD

Materials Needed:

Cardstock, red the sort I utilized has mica bits for a decent shimmer.

Watercolor computerized paper Free advanced paper pack

Printer quilling paper, red, 1/8"

Twill tape, white, 1/2"

Paper cut, red

Adornments pincers, 2 level nose

Hop rings, 2 silver

Clear message sticker

Glue stick

Paper shaper

Printer

Procedures

Stage 1: Score and overlap a 7½"x5½" bit of red cardstock to make a 3¾"x5½" card.

Stage 2: Print out the computerized watercolor background and slice it to quantify 3¼"x5". Utilize a glue stick to hold fast the square shape to the focal point of the card.

Stage 3: Outline the designed paper with quilling strips. Cover the strips unequivocally at the corners or miter at an inclination as appeared, following my instructional exercise.

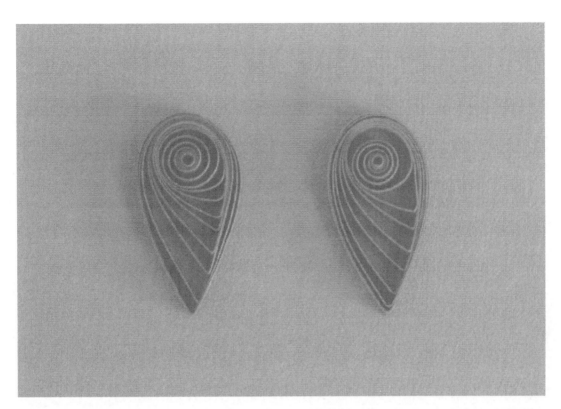

Stage 4: Make a heart (2 tears). Every tear requires a full-length strip, 24". Position the tears with the goal that the internal loops face a similar way. (This is inverse of how the sweets container tears were situated.) Facing the curls a similar way will give a decent look when forming the bend. Glue the tears one next to the other, nailing them set up to the work board until dry.

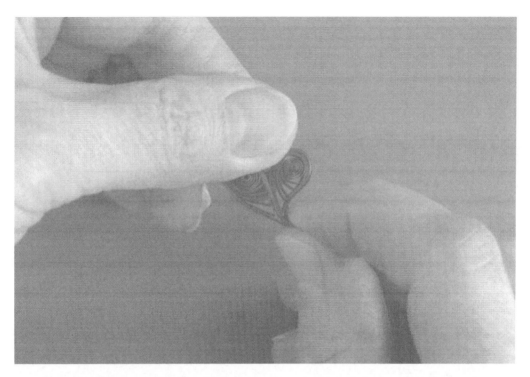

Stage 5: Grasp the tip of the heart and bend it tenderly.

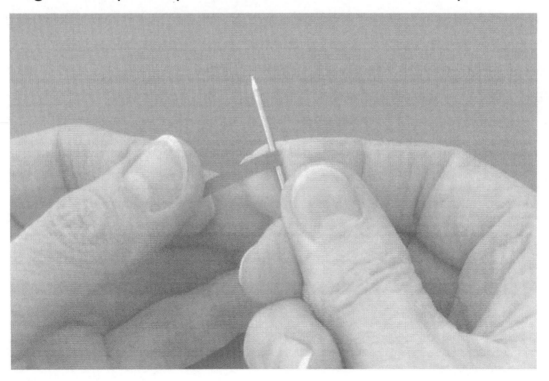

Stage 6: Roll a 2½" strip around the pole of a paper puncturing instrument or round toothpick to make a dot. Glue the torn end.

Tip: A torn end mixes superior to a blunt cut.

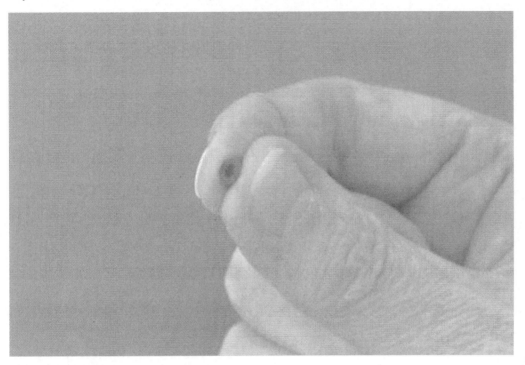

Stage 7: Pinch the dab to frame an oval ring loop.

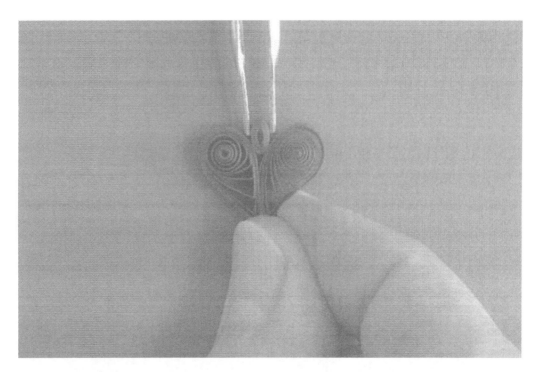

Glue the dab between the heart bends.

Stage 8: Use forceps to open two bounce rings and connect them to the ring curl.

Stage 9: Slip the bounce ring onto the paper cut.

Stage 10: Cut a ¾"- wide portion of cardstock to fit the width of the card between the circumscribed edges, and glue it set up, covering the lettering on the printed advanced paper.

Step11: Cut twill tape to a similar length as the cardstock strip. Slide the paper cut/heart onto the twill tape. Focus and glue the twill tape onto the cardstock strip.

Stage 12: Press on an unmistakable sticker message. I utilized "Praise"; within the message could peruse "our adoration" or "with the one you love." And obviously, Happy Valentine's Day!

As a variety, include a chain and wear the quilled heart as an accessory pendant. Whenever wanted, splash the heart with a glossy silk finish acrylic stain to give it water opposition and additional toughness.

Choosing the Right Paper for Quilling

As you should know by now, Quilling is all about paper, and so you should choose the right paper. Whenever you want to choose a quilling paper, there are many colors, creative finishes, and every type of gilded edged papers and pre-cut options.

Choosing a kind of paper that will be perfect for your quilling project can be difficult than cutting it with your hand. Purchasing a paper from quilling suppliers will mean that they will select a paper for you. Meanwhile, if you decide to buy it yourself, you will have to choose the paper.

Below are the tips on choosing the right paper

Choosing the Weight

The paper's weight, which is the thickness, has a big effect on how easy the paper will be to make. Marketable strips always come in writing weight, card stock, or text weight. Move through these options and choose the one you are comfortable with to choose the right paper.

Writing Weight

Writing weight paper, close to 20 pounds, is known as the lightest type. It is almost the same in thickness as the paper you would use in your printer, and it is more important for more important quilling. It is likely to cut easily if you use too much.

Text Weight

This particular paper is much heavier than the writing weight as it contains 60 to 80 pounds. It is the best option for new quilling projects such as jewelry. A much heavier paper such as this can stand up to stretch and added manipulation. However, if you need a traditional quilling look, you should go with a lighter weight.

Card Stock

This particular type is meant for quilling typography projects as well as outlining in mosaics. The card stock differs from 60 pounds weight to 110 pounds or higher. If you are using card stock, do not forget that the heavier the weight, the less quilling the paper will be. You have the option to coil and roll up Bristol weight card stock using a quilling tool. However, the cover stock is too thick and may not fit into a tool, and it will surely crack when finally rolled. The heavier weights are better options for gently curved and straight lines.

Selecting a Finish

There is no finish to the range of paper in the market. However, not every finish is effective for quilling projects, and that is why you should know what you want to get.

Metallic Paper

The metallic paper looks amazing, and major types are available in heavier text weight. A metallic paper may be easy to cut, but the smooth finish is difficult to glue, and so you may be needing a longer period to dry it, which means you have to be patient.

One-Sided Paper

If you have previously walked through the scrapbook walkway of any craft store close to you, perhaps, you might have had the option to quill with some of the wonderful papers kept there. One-sided paper can be an amazing choice for some projects, but do not forget that it is only the edge of the paper that displays in quilling. One-sided paper is always printed on white, which makes it not good for coils. However, it works perfectly well for outlining a shape.

Specialty Paper

Specialty paper can be exciting to use, but few are much better than others for cutting at home. The paper you can see above is produced from real cherry wood. It is attractive but a little difficult to cut. Look into the particular qualities of the paper you are arranging to use when you are selecting your cutting tools and surface.

Vat-Dyed Colored Paper

It is important to know that the vat-dyed paper is the easiest to cut. Also, it is the easiest to quill as well as not difficult to find at any store. Colored paper can be amazing for a majority of quilling projects. But make sure you select a colorfast paper and an acid-free paper. Since quilling takes a lot of time, your creative pieces should also be able to last for a long time.

Finding the Correct Length

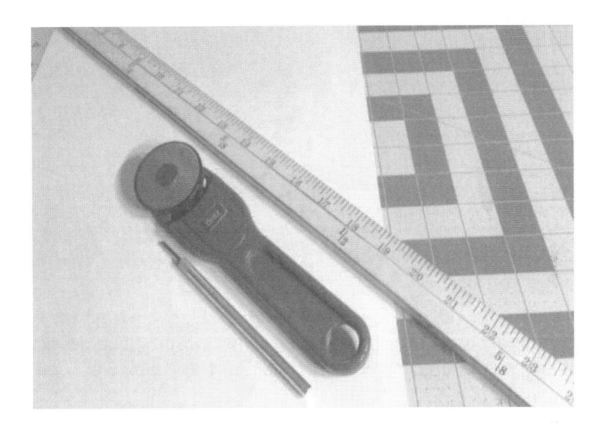

The length of your paper is also important when choosing the right paper for quilling. The standard length is 8.5 by 11-inch size is everywhere in stores, but most quilling patterns use strips that are 17 inches or more. If you can locate the larger size, you will have an easy time following away. But if you do not, just make use of a little glue to get the correct length.

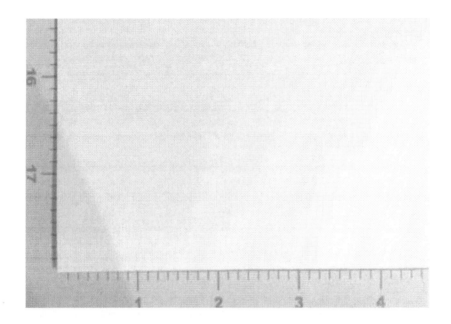

You can also make your own Quilling Paper, which will be perfect for you. To do this, there are a couple of things you will need. They include:

1. Ruler or yardstick

2. Self-healing mat or suitable cutting surface

3. Craft knife or rotary cutter

4. Paper of choice

- **Square Up Your Edges**

While making use of the ruler on your self-healing mat, proceed to square up the edges on the left-hand side of your paper sheet.

- **Trim Away the Excess**

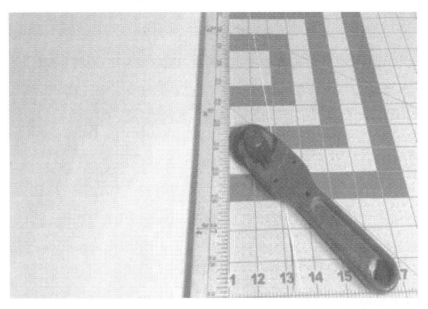

Make use of your yardstick to square up the other side of your paper. Sheets are not always cut well, which means you will have to trim off the surplus before you begin cutting. Make use of a rotary cutter than a utility knife to trim away the excess.

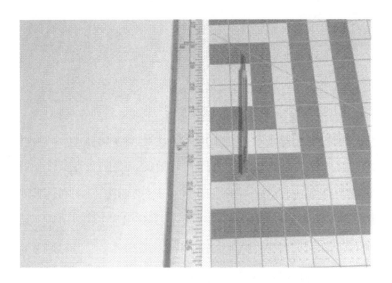

- **Line it Up**

While holding your paper safely, take your yardstick to the left. Be aware that the preset markings on the self-healing mat will provide you the width you need when you decide to cut.

- **Cut Your Strip**

If you are using a rotary tool to cut, you may find it easier to start at the bottom and move up. But with a utility knife, starting from up may be true. Always endeavor to lean heavily into the yardstick with your body's weight and hand to prevent falling as you cut.

Paper Quilling Greetings Cards

Expressing heartfelt gratitude or making an unexpected marriage proposal—all of these sentiments and more can be hidden inside one small card using the techniques described in this section. Send cards designed with lavender teardrop flowers, and your loved ones will cherish the quilled card you designed just for them.

Valentine's Day

PINK AND LIGHT PURPLE BUNNY EAR FLOWERS

Make four pink and four light purple bunny ear flowers, using ½ length strips.

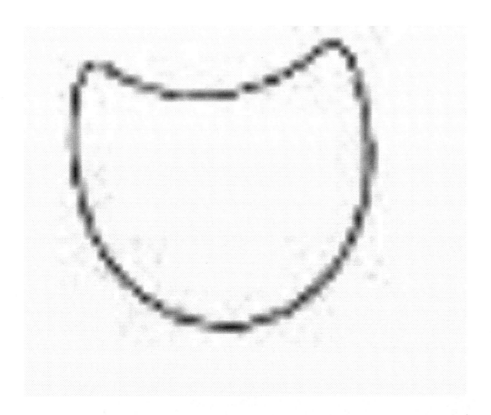

STEMS WITH LEAVES

Prepare yellow, green strips ½ (1.3 cm) longer than a ¼ length strip. Roll marquises using the ¼ length only. Glue each marquise and use the remaining length as the stem. Make eight marquises using ¼ length yellow, green strips—glue one marquise to each stem.

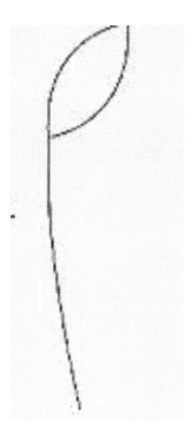

VINES

Make eighty V scrolls, using 1/6 length white strips.

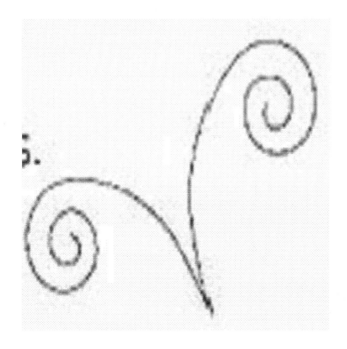

YELLOW MARQUISE FLOWER BUDS

Make eight marquises, using 1/8 length yellow strips

HEART

Make a 5/8'' (1.6) diameter circle by winding a yellow strip twice. To make a heart shape, pinch one end of the circle to make a pointed end and push the opposite ends inward, using a needle tool. Make five loose scrolls, using 3/4 '' (1.9 cm) long yellow and canary yellow strips, and use them to fill the inside of the heart.

ASSEMBLY

1.   Glue eight stems with leaves to form a (6 cm) diameter circle.

2.   Glue the vines and yellow marquise flower buds.

3.   Glue the pink and light purple bunny ear flowers between the leaves, and add the heart to the wreath center.

4.   Use tweezers for creating the small shapes in this project.

HAPPY BIRTHDAY 1

RIBBON

Make two bunny eras and two arrowheads, using full length grape purple strips. Wrap the centre of the ribbon with a 1/8'' (3 mm) wide strip.

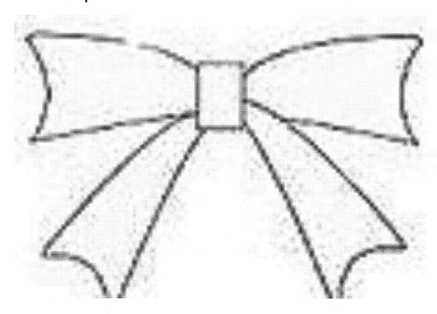

LAVENDER MARQUISE FLOWER AND FLOWER BUDS

Make four flowers for each flower. Roll three marquises, using 1/6 length lavender strips. Make six more marquises for buds.

LAVENDER TIGHT COIL FLOWER BBUDS

Make four tight coils using 1/8 lavender strips.

LEAVES

Make fourteen large and six small leaves. For each leaf, make three-loop vertical husking using moss green strips. Make four more leaves. For each leaf, make two-loop vertical husking.

VINES

Make six loose scrolls with ¼ length yellow-green strips and two more with 1/6 length yellow-green strips.

POLLEN

Make six tight coils, using 1/16 length canary yellow strips.

HEART-SHAPED STEM

Fold one (21 cm) long moss green strip in half and curve the ends inward. Glue the ends together to form a heart shape.

ASSEMBLY

1.   Glue the heart-shaped stem in the center of the card.

2.   Glue the large leaves outside the bottom of the heart-shaped stem and glue the small leaves above them.

3.   Glue the lavender marquise flowers outside the heart stem and between the leaves. Glue the vines on the inside of the heart shape.

4.   Glue the pollen between the flowers and leaves. Add the ribbon in the center of the heart shape.

5.   Add a happy birthday to the center of the card.

WISHES AND LOVE

WHITE MARQUISE FLOWERS

Make four flowers. For each flower, make seven marquises, using ¼ length white strips. Then roll a tight coil, using a 1/16'' (1.6 mm) wide 1/5 length canary yellow strip and glue it to the center of the flower.

TURQUOISE BUNNY EAR FLOWERS

Make four flowers, for each flower, make four bunny ears, using 1/3 length turquoise strips. Then roll a tight coil, using a ¼'' (1.9 cm) long yellow strip, and glue it inside the flower centre.

STEMS WITH LEAVES

Prepare kiwi paper strips 3/8'' (1 cm) longer than a 1/6 length strip. Roll marquises, using the 1/6 length only. Glue the marquise, and use the remaining 3/5'' (1 cm) as the stem. Make marquises, using 1/5 length kiwi strips, and glue one to each stem. Make four stems with leaves.

VINES AND LEAVES

Make vines using 1/6 length kiwi strips. Make marquises, using 1/6 length kiwi strips, and glue them to the vines.

PASTEL PURPLE TIGHT COILS

Make eight tight coils, using 1/8 length pastel purple strips.

RIBBON

Make a ribbon, using a ¼'' (6 mm) wide by '' (6.4 cm) long pastel purple strip, as shown in the picture.

POLLEN

Stick lavender strips to a piece of double-sided tape and cut eighteen triangles.

ASSEMBLY

    1.   Glue the white marquise flowers to form a (5.4 cm) diameter circle. Add the turquoise flowers between the white flowers.

    2.   Glue the vines and leaves between the white and turquoise flowers.

3.   Glue the pastel purple tight coils between the leaves. Add the ribbon to the center of the wreath.

4.   Glue nine lavender pollen pieces above and below the wreath.

MEMORIES OF SPRING

CANARY YELLOW TEARDROP FLOWERS

Make eight elongated teardrops, using ½ -length canary yellow strips: glue 3/8" (1cm)-long light green strips to make stems.

WHITE BUNNY EAR FLOWERS

Make eight bunny ears using 1/6 –length white strips. Glue a 3/8" (1-cm)-long light green strip to each for stems.

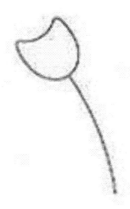

LEAVES

Make sixteen marquises with a single curved end, using 1/5-length light green strips.

WREATH FRAME

Make a two ¼" (5.7cm) –diameter frame by winding an olive green strip four times

BUTTERFLY

To make a body of the butterfly, roll a marquise using a ¼ -¼-length yellow strip. Make two triangles, using full-length yellow strips for upper wings. Make two triangles, using ⅔-length canary yellow strips for the bottom wings. Glue the wings to the body and add antennae.

ASSEMBLY

1.   Glue the wreath frame in the center of the card. Glue the canary yellow teardrop flowers and white bunny ear flowers proportionally around the wreath.

2.   Glue the leaves between the flowers and glue the butterfly in the center.

3.   **MOTHER'S DAY**

LAVENDER TEARDROP FLOWERS

Make four flowers, for each flower, make five teardrops, using ⅓-length lavender strips. Then roll a tight coil, using a ⅛-length canary yellow strip, and glue it to the flower centre.

WHITE BUNNY EAR FLOWERS

Make four flowers. For each flower, make four bunny ears, using ⅓-length white strips. Make tight coils, using ⅛-length canary yellow strips, and glue them to the flower centres

LEAVES AND STEMS

Make eight marquises with single curved end, using ¼ -length kiwi strips. Make stems, using ½" (1.3 cm) –long light green strips.

VINES

Make eight vines, using ⅙- length yellow strips.

ASSEMBLY

1. Glue four lavender flowers to form a 2" (5.1 cm) –diameter circle.

2. Glue the white bunny ear flowers between the lavender flowers, and add the stems.

3. Glue the leaves and vines.

HAPPY BIRTHDAY II

FRINGED FLOWERS

Make two fringed flowers. For each flower, fringe ¼" (6 mm) – wide by 7⅛" (20 cm) –long bright blue strips, roll tightly and glue the end. Spread out the fringed ends.

TURQUOISE TEARDROP FLOWERS

Make four flowers. Make each flower with five teardrops, using ⅓-length turquoise strips. Make tight coils, using ⅕" (1.6 mm) wide ⅛-length yellow strips, and glue them to the flower centers.

FLOWER BUDS AND STEMS

Make four flower buds, using ¼ -¼-length lavender stripes, and prepares four 1⅝" (4 cm) –long olive green strips for stems.

LIGHT PURPLE BUNNY-EAR FLOWERS AND LEAVES

Make eight bunny ears, using ¼ -¼-length light purple stripes.

Make eight marquises, using ¼ -¼-length moss green strips.

LARGE LEAVES AND VINES

Make two leaves. For each leaf, make three teardrops, using ¼ -¼-length olive green strips. Make eight loose scrolls, using ¼ -¼-length olive green and turquoise stripes.

POLLEN

Sticks canary yellow paper to a piece of double-sided tape and cut out ten triangles.

ASSEMBLY

1. Glue one of the fringed flowers on the upper left side and the other on the bottom right side.

2. Glue the four flower buds and stems to each side of the fringed flowers. Add the bunny ear flowers and vines.

3. Glue the turquoise teardrop flowers on each side of the fringed flowers. Add the large leaves and vines.

4. Finish with the pollen.

WHITE TEARDROP FLOWER

Make the flower with six teardrops, using ½ -length white strips. Make a tight coil, using a marquise canary yellow strip, and glue it to the flower centre. Attach the teardrops, using ¼ length light green strips, and marquise scrolls, using ⅛-length yellow strips.

TURQUOISE BUNNY EAR FLOWER

Make the flower four bunny ears, with ½ -½-length turquoise strips. Make a coil using ¼ -length white strips; place it to the flower center.

Make two marquises, using ⅛-length white strips.

CANARY YELLOW MARQUISE FLOWER

Make right marquise, using ½ -length canary yellow strips. Make a right coil, using ⅓ -⅓-length sage green strips, and glue the flower center. For a stem, prepare one 2⅛" (5.4 cm) with an olive-green strip and curve it slightly. Make two marquise sage using ½ -, and ¼ -length moss green strips.

ASSEMBLY

1. Glue 2" x 2" (5.1 x 5.1 cm) pieces of light yellow and jade paper on the left side of the card and a 4 ½" x 2 " (11.3 x 5.1cm) pieces of light yellow and jade paper on the right side.

2. Using spray glue, glue a 4 ½" x 4 ¼" (11.5 x 11.5cm) piece of tracing paper on top of the pieces in step 1.

3. Glue the white teardrop flower on the light yellow piece of paper. Glue the turquoise bunny ear flower on the jade piece of paper. Add the leaves and vines.

4. Glue the canary yellow flower on the lilac paper, and glue the leaves and the stem.

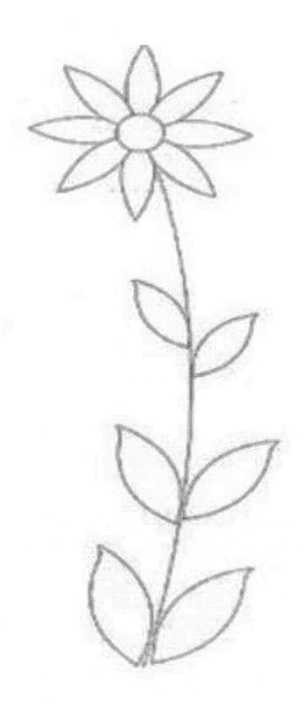

5. ANNIVERSARY

CANARY YELLOW TEARDROPS FLOWER

Make one flowers. For each flower, make eight elongated teardrops using ⅓-length yellow strips. Then roll a canary using ¼ - length yellow strip and glue it to the flower centre.

YELLOW TEARDROP FLOWERS

Make four flowers. For each flower, make five teardrops, using ¼ -length yellow strips. Then roll a tight coil, using a length orange strip, and glue it to the centre of the flower.

CANARY YELLOW FLOWER BUDS

Make two flowers. For each flower, make three marquises with single curved end, using ¼ -length canary yellow strips. Make two canary ears, using ¼ -length moss green using the flower cups.

WHITE FLOWERS WITH CENTER

Make the flowers. Make a tight coil with ½ -length yellow strips for each flower and wrap it twice with a fringed of (4.3 mm) wide white strip.

WHITE LEAVES

Make the wide leaves with three small leaves each. For each small plate, make three marquises, using ¼ -¼-length moss green strips, and glue them together. Glue them together. Glue the three small leaves together to make on a wide leaf.

LEAVES

Make two leaves. Make three marquises with double curved ends for each leaves, using ⅓-length moss green strips, and glue them together.

ASSEMBLY

1. Draw a 2 ½" (6.4 cm) –diameter circle in the center.

2. Glue the two canary teardrops flower facing each other. Make two groups of three white flowers and glue them facing each other.

3. Glue two yellow teardrops flower to one side of each of the three white flower groups. Add the wide leaves next to the flowers.

4. Glue stems to the flowers bud and positions them between the canary yellow and white flowers.

5. Make the letters "LOVE" and glue them to the center.

6. Make the letters "LOVE" and glue them to the center.

Paper Quilling Designs for Framing

The process in this section will yield beautiful frame-able pieces for en-living the décor of any room in your home; given as gifts, they will recall the small flowers of early spring, newly blossoming violets, or perhaps, a birthday bouquet given long ago that is now a lasting reminder of that special time. From simple designs for beginners to complicated designs requiring some experience, these projects will expose you to limitless paper quill possibilities.

Yellow wildflower

A good project for beginners, this project is done with marquises. It is suitable for greeting cards or small frames.

YELLOW MARQUISE FLOWER

Make a flower with eight ovals, using ½ length yellow strips. Make a tight coil, using a ½ length white strip. Glue the coil to the centre of the flower.

LEAVES AND STEM FOR YELLOW FLOWER

Layer one olive green and one khaki strip together. Fold the strips in a zigzag pattern as seen in fig. 1, press the pattern together, and apply glue to the leaf's inside. Make four leaves as seen in fig. 2. Glue the leaves to a 3'' (7.5 cm) long moss green strip.

ORANGE MARQUISE FLOWER

For a flower center, make a marquise using a 1/3 length dusty yellow strip. Make seven off-center marquises, using ½ length orange strips. Place the orange marquises below the flower center and glue them tightly together. To make stamens, use five 1/32 (0.8mm) wide and 3/8 (1 cm) long yellow strips. Roll the ends to the center of the strips. Glue the stamens above the flower's center.

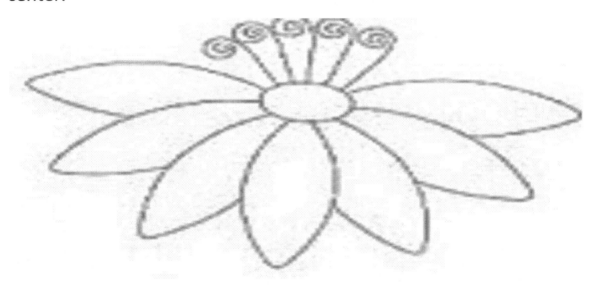

LEAVES AND STEM FOR ORANGE FLOWER

Make three marquises, using 2/5 length moss green strips. Make three more, using ½ length moss green strips. Alternately glue the leaves to a (7cm) long olive green stem.

PURPLE TEARDROP FLOWER

Make a teardrop using a full-length purple strip; wrap a light purple stripe around it twice. Glue five petals together to form the flower. Make a tight coil, using a 1/3 length canary yellow strip, and glue the coil to the center of the flower

LEAVES AND STEM FOR PURPLE FLOWER

Make four off-center marquises, using 2/5 length olive green strips. Make four more, using ½ length olive green strips. Attach the leaves in pairs on opposite sides of a slightly curved (8.2Cm) long khaki stem.

PINK BUNNY RED FLOWER

Using ½ length strips, Make three pinks and three light pink bunny ears, make a tight coil, Using a 1/3 length kiwi strip, And glue it to the center of the flower

LEAVES AND STEM FOR PINK FLOWER

Make six big leaves and two small leaves from moss green three-loop vertical husking's. Alternatively, glue the leaves to a 3 (7.5) long khaki stem.

LAVENDER TEARDROP FLOWER

Make six teardrops, using ½ length lavender strips, and glue them together. Make a tight coil, use a ¼ length orange strip, and glue it to the flower's center.

LEAVES AND STEM FOR LAVENDER FLOWER

Make three leaves. For each leaf, roll three marquises, using 1/3 length khaki strips. Make two more leaves. For each leaf, roll three marquises from 1/3 length olive green strips. Alternatively, glue the leaves to a (6.5 cm) long olive green stem.

ASSEMBLY

1.   Glue the purple flower in the center.

2.   Glue the pink and lavender flowers on the right side and the orange and yellow flowers on the left.

Violet Bouquet

To make the flowers stand out, this project uses teardrop flowers wrapped with strips of the same bright color family. The rich yellow ribbon and purple flower combination especially bring out the essence of paper quilling. This project can be used to make greeting cards, or it can be applied to small frames.

PURPLE TEARDROP FLOWERS

Make fifteen teardrops, using ½ length purple strips. Wrap each teardrop once with bright blue. Make three flowers, using five teardrops for each. Make a tight coil, use a 1/3 length yellow strip, and glue the coil to the flower center.

LIGHT PURPLE MARQUISE FLOWER

Make five flowers for each flower; make three marquises, using ¼ length light purple stripes.

FLOWER CUP AND LEAVES

Prepare two (2.5cm) long moss green strips. Glue the two strips together, leaving (16 cm) unglued, cut the unglued ends to make them pointy. Make five flower cups by slightly curving the pointy ends. Glue the light purple flowers to the flowers cups. Make teardrops, using ¼ length olive green strips. Glue two teardrops to each stem.

LEAVES

Make four leaves with three teardrops each, one teardrop from a ½ length olive green strip and two teardrops from 1/3 length sage green strips. Make an additional two teardrops. Using ½ -length sage green strips.

RIBBON

Make two bunny ears and two arrowheads using full-length canary yellow strips. Glue these together, as shown in the picture.

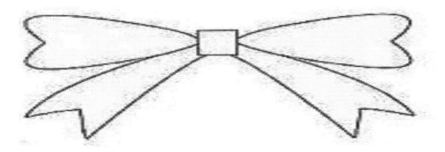

STEMS

Make stems, using nine slightly curved 1'' (2.5 cm) long sage green strips.

POLLEN

Stick a bright paper strip to one side of a piece of double-sided tape. Cut eight small triangles

ASSEMBLY

1. Glue the three purple teardrop flowers in the centre.

2. Glue the light purple flowers around the purple teardrop flowers proportionally.

3. Glue the leaves in the spaces between the light purple flowers.

4.   Glue the nine stems below the purple teardrop flowers and attach the ribbon just above them.

5.   Decorate the empty spaces with the pollen shapes.

A Basket of Flowers

This is a very useful project for learning how to weave a basket pattern. Various types of baskets and textures can be created by using different width paper strips and colours. In this project, a three dimensional look is created by using marquises, fringed flowers and teardrops.

PASTEL GREEN MARQUISE FLOWERS

Make eight flowers. For each one, make six marquises, using 1/3 length pastel green strips. Make tight coils, using ¼ and 1/6 length yellow strips. Use the coils for flower centres.

TANGERINE TEARDROP FLOWER

Make four flowers. For each flower, make five teardrops, using ¼ length tangerine strips. Make tight coils, using 1/6 length strips. Use the coils for flower centres.

FRINGED FLOWERS

Make five fringed flowers, using 7/3 x 6'' (6 x 15 cm) paper strips.

STEM WITH LEAVES

Make forty to fifty marquises, each with a single curved end. Glue five to seven of them to each 2'' 5 cm long stem. Make a total of seven stems with leaves.

BASKET

Prepare eight 1/16'' (5 mm) wide by 9/2'' (11.5 cm) long whit strips and twenty five 1/8'' (3 mm) wide by (7.2 cm) long whit strips. Glue eight of the (5mm) wide strips vertically every 1/16 (1.6 mm) across. Start weaving by alternately inserting the 1/3'' (3 mm) wide strips (see fig. 1). When the woven piece reaches 19/8'' x 3'' (6 x 7.5 cm), apply glue on top of it and allow it to dry. Cut a basket shape from a thick piece of paper, using a template, and glue it to the woven piece. Trim the woven piece leaving a margin for folding (see fig.2) . Fold the margin back so that it has the shape of a basket and glue it (see fig. 3). Make two spirals, using 1/16'' (1`.6 mm) wide by (8 cm) long white strips. Glue the spirals to the top and bottom of the basket.

ASSEMBLY

1.	Glue the basket in the lower center.

2.	Glue six pastel green flowers (opposite page).

3.	Glue the four fringed flowers in the remaining spaces. Place one fringed flower on top of a pastel green flower.

4.	Glue four tangerine flowers and two pastel green flowers on top of the other flowers for a three-

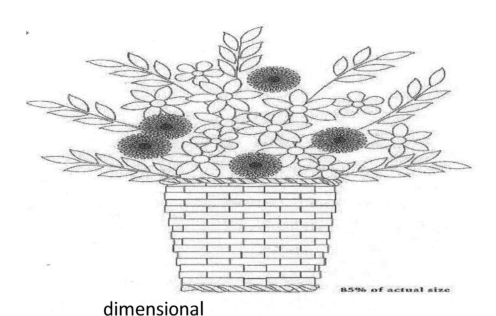

85% of actual size

dimensional

YELLOW TEARDROP FLOWER

Make four flowers. For each flower, use a needle tool to make the tight coils with a centre hole, using 1/8 length yellow strips. Glue four coils together to form one flower

LARGE LEAVES

Make two marquises with single curved, Using a ½ length olive green strips, and three more, using ½ length moss green strips

SMALL LEAVES

Make a marquise with single curved end, using a 1'4 length olive green strip, and one more, using a ¼ length moss green strip.

RIBBON

Prepare one ¼'' (6 mm) wide by 17/2'' (5.4 cm) long (upper ribbon layer) and one (16 mm) wide by (6 cm) long ribbon layer) grass green paper strip. Fold both in half to mark the centre of the strips. Fold the ends toward the centre and glue them. Glue the upper

Layer and lower layer together, and wrap the center with a 5/16 '' (8 mm) wide full length bright green strip. Prepare a ¼'' (6 mm) wide by 8.2 cm) long bright green paper strip. Make a small cut in the center to allow the ends to bend downward. Cut a V shape into both ends of the ribbon. Glue it to the center of the ribbon.

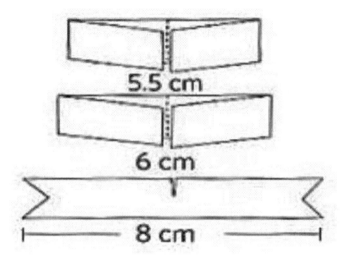

STEMS

Make four spirals with (5.7 cm) long light green paper strips. Cut each to 13/8'' (4 cm) long.

ASSEMBLY

1. Glue three bright blue bunny ear flowers in the centre. Glue nine small blue marquise flowers above them.

2. Glue three yellow teardrop flowers on the left side and one more on the right side.

3. Glue the large and small leaves in the empty spaces.

4. Glue the spiral stems below the right blue bunny ear flowers. Add the ribbon on top of the stems.

Flowers in spring

This project uses petals made from three or four elements and has a delicate and lifelike quality. It has a high level of difficulty and requires quilling experience. The leaves are also made with several marquises bunched and glued together.

YELLOW FLOWERS

Make twenty-four flowers. For each flower, make five-light coils with a centre hole, using 1/8 length yellow strips.

STEMS

Prepare five 5'' (12.7 cm) long moss green strips. Glue them together, leaving (1 cm) from the end unglued, spread the unglued ends. Glue five yellow flowers above the spread ends, and glue six more yellow flowers above those. Repeat to make a total of two stems.

PURPLE FLOWERS

Make angled marquises with full-length purple strips. Wrap a moss green strip twice each. Make three petal flowers.

STEMS

Glue five 4'' (10 cm) long moss green strips together and the upper portion. Make a wide or narrow bend in the stems, according to the desired position of the purple flower.

YELLOW FLOWER WRAPPED IN WHITE STRIPS

Make two half moon shapes. Fold a 5/16 (8 mm) long tangerine strip in half, connect a ½ length yellow strip, and then make a four loop vertical husking. To form the petal, position the strips between two half moons. Wrap the finished petal with a half length white strip, leaving some space at the tips of the petals.

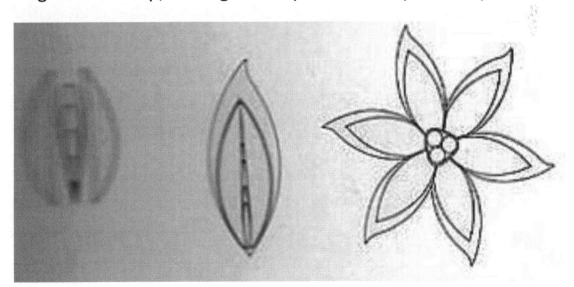

FLOWER CENTRE

After making three tight coils, using 1/8 length yellow strips, wrap them three times with a light green strip.

STEMS

Make stems by giving five (5.4 cm) long strips together.

LEAVES

Roll about ninety marquises with double curved ends, using ½ length moss green and sage green stripes. Connect eight of the marquises together to form a row, and then do the same for another seven. Glue the two rows of leaves together. Before the glue dries completely, use your hands to form a leaf shape. Wrap the leaf with a moss green strip.

ASSEMBLY

1. Position one yellow flower in the upper center and the other slightly lower.

2. Glue leaves to the right and left of the yellow flowers. Glue the purple flowers, placing the stems in between the leaves.

3. Place the yellow flower wrapped in white strips on top of the purple flower. Add the stems and leaves.

Simple Practical Projects to Perfect Your Quilling Skills

How to Make Paper Quills Butterfly

Art is naturally appealing, and paper quills butterfly is an art. Therefore, paper quills butterfly is appealing to not just the eye but the mind. However, there seems to be something that ignites a deeper sense of artistic elegance in paper quills butterfly.

If you know how to make paper quills butterfly, you sure would be among the finest artists in the world. Would you not love to be regarded a fine artist? I see you want to. Now, I will introduce you to the basics and equally expose the secret things that could make your paper quills butterfly unique.

Required Materials for Paper Quills Butterfly

To arrive at a decent paper quills butterfly, there are a few materials to put in place. The basic five materials include:

1. The quilling paper
2. Quilling pins
3. Quilling stencil
4. Slotted quilling tool
5. Dispensing quilling glue

If you do not have any of the aforementioned tools, the chances of arriving at something elegant would be quite low. Some persons substitute for other papery materials as a replacement for the traditional quilling paper. But then, the result would either be a distorted finishing or a swaying design.

How to Make Paper Quill Butterflies

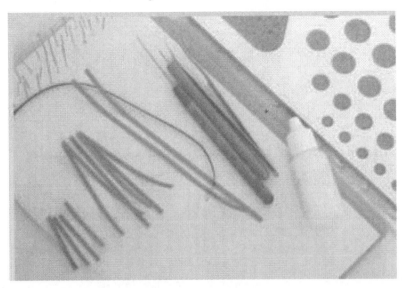

1. Gather the Required Supplies

For a small butterfly, the required supplies include:

- (4) One and a half inch strips
- (6) Three-inch strips
- (2) Six-inch strips
- 12-inch strip of black slotted quilling tool glue

#Optional Tools

- Needle tool
- Tweezers
- Circle sizing board
- Corkboard and pins

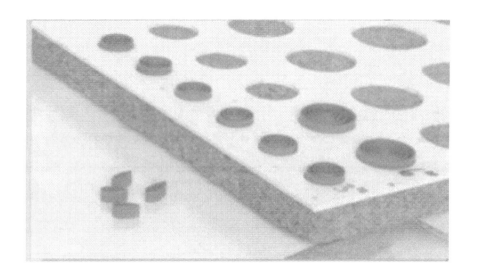

2. Fold the Strips in the Corkboard

After you have the mentioned tools in place, punch holes on the corkboard. The hole may not necessarily have to be like what you have on this photo. You may design however way you desire. In this photo, a pink strip is used because it is what I choose. There are more lovely colors and if you do not mind, I will recommend some colors for you. You may go for something like royal blue, pitch color, or emerald green if you love pink, no problem.

3. Arrange the Strips as Shown Here

At this point, take a studying look at the image above. You can see the looks of the quills. Now, here is how to achieve the design. I believe you have the glue with you because it is needed now. Just as in the picture above, arrange each pink (depending on the color you are using) strip to look the same. Once you have been able to do so, apply the quilling glue and try not to hold the bottom of the strap tight. Since it may be difficult not to hold it while applying the glue, hold it with less pressure so that each wing would be pointy when the glue is dry.

Introduction to Paper Quilling – Christmas Wreath

The Christmas wreath paper quilling is a definition of artistic elegance. It could be designed to be smaller as well as double the size or big. What determines its size is simply the height age quantity of paper strips used. In essence, you can realize any Christmas quilling size you desire and tweak the strips to whatever concept is required.

I will share the best practice towards coming up with an unbeatable Christmas wreath. Just be attentive to the text and picture details of this content. Moreover, you should create something pleasant at the end of this tutorial on how to make a Christmas wreath paper quilling.

Christmas wreath is one of the few most fancied paper quilling designs. It costs just attentiveness and a little time before a novice can become an expert. Also, do not forget to make your color choices match the occasion. As you can see in the photos, there is a dominant combination of green and red paper stripes to compliment.

Ready to make your first cute Christmas wreath paper quilling? Then, let's get started so you can share your design with the world on time.

Materials Required for Christmas Wreath Paper Quilling

- Two green paper strips of 1½ inch long
- Three red paper strips of 1½ inch long
- 22 green paper strips of 3 inches long
- Paper glue

- Corkboard

- Scissors

- Circular guide board

- Quilling tool (toothpick is an alternative)

- Tweezers

Beginners Guide for a Christmas Wreath Paper Quilling

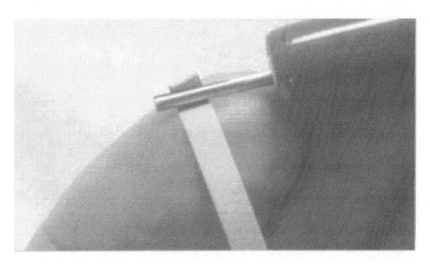

The 22 Green Strips

As in the picture above, pick and place a green stripe on the referral finger. Whether you are left-handed or right-handed, use the quilling tool or toothpick to spin the strip around.

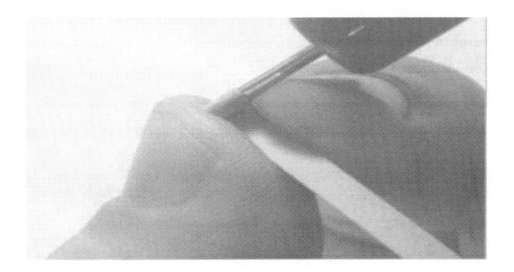

Keep tying the strip around and ensure it is firm enough for a good result.

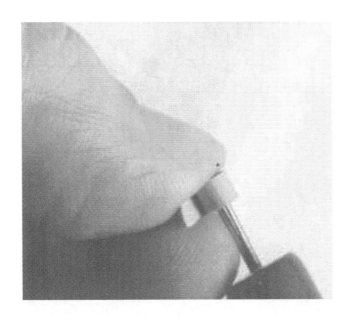

Remember to place the strip at the tip of the quilling tool. This will help the strip maintain its shape the moment it is taken off.

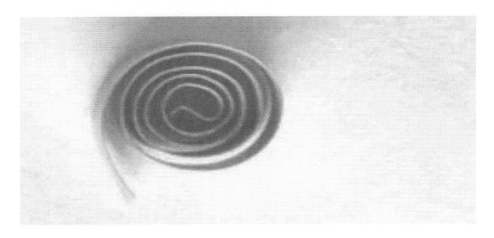

In the end, you should have a structure similar to the image above.

Once the strip is withdrawn from the quilling tool's tip, it will unfold a bit in a spiral form or coil form. If you're following this guide, the number of coiled strips should be 22.

Remember, I mentioned 22 green strips 3 inches long.

The 3 Red Strips

Pick up a paper strip and scissors and cut through the paper as shown above.

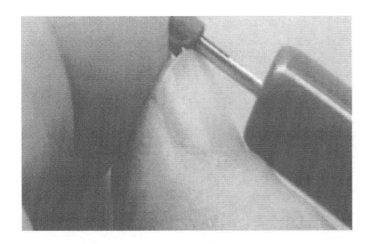

You will be left with three strips. For this guide, 3 strips are what are required. However, do not make 3 strips if your Christmas wreath is bigger or smaller.

Coil each strip firmly around the quilling tool. While releasing, you should have 3 perfect loosed coiled strips. If the coils are not spiral enough, tie them again round the tip of the quilling tool, toothpick or whatever alternative tool.

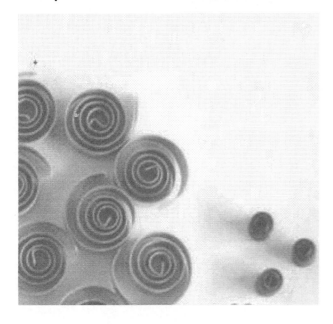

Finally, you may arrange the strips as found above. Remember, the more coiling each strip is, the better for the entire design. Place your loosed coils and optionally take photos of them.

Shaping the Green Coils

The green coils or coiled strips must now be shaped for results using paper glue.

It is often problematic to get each coil to be perfect in size. As seen in the photo 'A' above, there are two coils with both being unequal. If you continue making Christmas wreath paper quilling with unequal loosed coils such as the above, the result will not be desirable. Let's see what can be done to obtain equal coils.

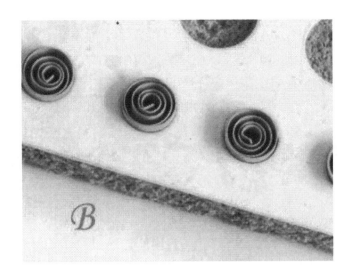

In photo 'B', you can see that the coils are all equal. This also means that I will have a perfect wreathing. In order to make equal coils, I recommend using a ruler, precisely a ruler with hole. With the hole, it will be super easy to stencil the strips to equal shapes and sizes.

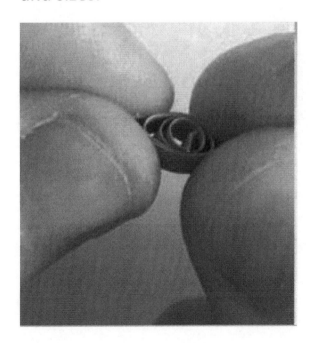

When you are pleased with your coils' shapes and sizes, carefully and firmly press two opposite ends of the coils to give you an 'eye' shape. You may press as firmly as you like but do not soil the strip. Repeat this for all coils.

You should have 22 eye-shaped coils of green colors and 6 non-eye-shaped rolls of red color strips. Note, the number of strips here are only applicable to this guide. Do not be confused since it may differ from your size of quill.

Arranging Wreaths Together

Now, you require the paper glue. Look at the photo above carefully. You have seen how those eye-shaped coils are being placed together, right? You have to produce the same design in order not to mess up the Christmas wreath. First, pick two coils and place them exactly the same way it is on the picture. That is, only the near-middle area of both coils must be glued to each other.

Repeat the process by bringing in more coils. The added paper glue must not be excessive in order not to distort the appearance.

When carefully and correctly done, you should have something similar to the above photo.

If need be, before the glue dries, place the wreathed coils on the corkboard or whatever is being used. Now, place pins on portions that look a bit distorted. As can be seen on the photo, five pins are being placed to readjust some portions.

Applying Embellishments

Apply at least two drops of paper glue to the beautification material. The glue must be applied on the underneath part of the material to be placed. Immediately, use tweezers to pick and place the material on the preferred portion of the wreath. In the absent of tweezers, you may use your fingers but I find it convenient using tweezers to place embellishments.

Do you intend making earrings? If so, pick up the 1½ inch green strips and roll them using the quilling tool.

Now, apply paper glue to eye-shaped marquis. Apply the glue across the embellishment initially applied.

As seen above, your beautiful Christmas wreath paper quilling is ready. Go on and send them through to loved ones. The interesting aspect of this is that you get to spend less or no money at all in sending something artistic and pleasing to the senses to people.

Using this idea, you can come up with a larger quilling. All you need to do is to increase the sizes from what is stated here. If you require something far smaller, reduce the strip sizes, and you will have exactly what you desire. Not to flatter, although Christmas wreaths are fine, the maker or artist who makes an attractive Christmas wreath is finer.

Apart from making these quills into Christmas cards, you could well make them into earrings. However, you would have to apply sealants since paper quills are very delicate. You may not require sealant for a Christmas card, but you definitely do require sealant when making it for earring.

Moreover, you do not have to rummage the wreaths and marquise with excess sealants. A simple dressing would be enough in order not to cause the coils to stay loosed. When it dries, reapply sealant again, this time all over, and make sure it sticks well to the wreaths; otherwise, it won't be nice for the earring.

How to Make Paper Quilled Daisy Earring

You know, paper quilling comprises quite a number of mouth-watering designs. All of these designs evolve with time and become even better depending on the creativity and craftiness of the person or artist handling it.

Earrings look good but using paper quilling concept makes it look better. The daisy earring from paper quilling stands a chance against diamond-plaited sorts of earrings. And, this would solely depend on the making and finishing. Together, let us uncover the appropriate way on how to make paper quilled daisy. The moment you coat with sealants, trust me, everyone would definitely give it a second look. Ready to be proud of your craftiness? Then, follow this simple guide and be attentive to the photos.

Required Materials Paper Quilling Flowers

- A slotted quilling tool

- Quilling paper

- Quilling stencil

- Pins

- Paper glue

- Glue dispenser

How to Make Paper Quilled Flower Materials

Below are the basic materials required to do paper quilled flower on your own. Refer to the photo if you can't identify of the materials.

- 5 paper strips (6 inches long)

- Another 5 paper strips (3 inches long)

- Slotted quilling tool

- Paper glue

- Corkboard

- Pins

- A circle-sizing tool (It may be a board as well with hole)

The strips may be any preferred color as long as it suits the occasion.

1. Gluing Both Strips

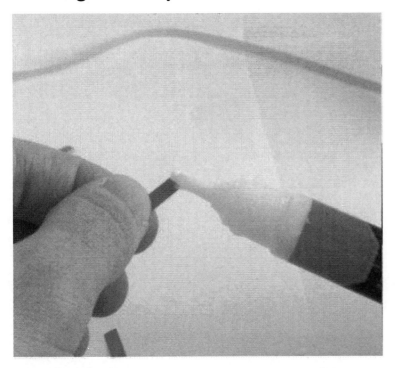

Apply paper glue at the preferred edges of each strip (3" and 6").

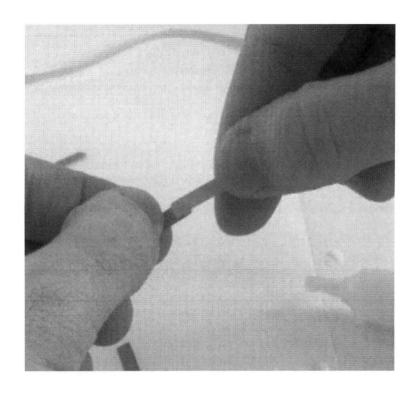

Bring the edges of each strip where you applied glue. Note, the strips you are gluing together must not be the same inches i.e. only 3" strips must be paired with 6" strips.

2. Rolling the Quilling Paper

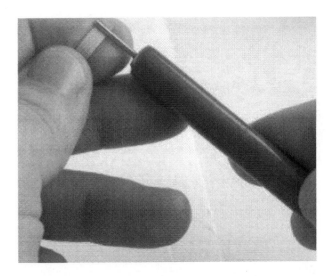

Pick up the slotted quilling tool. Place one edge of the glued strips at the tip of the tool.

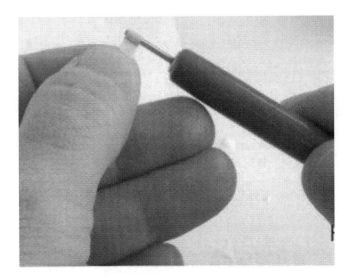

Start turning the quilling tool.

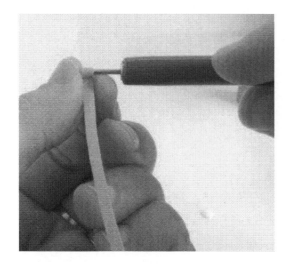

Ensure that you hold firm but not tight.

Go gently and keep rolling until the entire length of the strip is consumed.

3. Remove the Quilling Tool

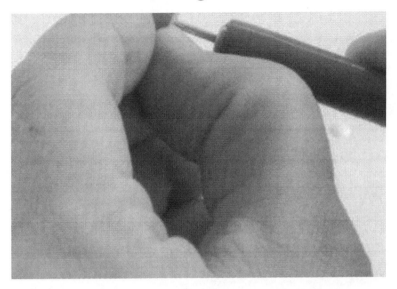

Add a light pressure using your forehand and thumb to press the strip to the quilling tool.

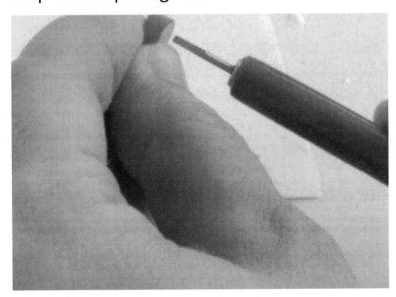

Carefully remove the scrolled paper from the quilling tool or whatever you're using. Ensure that the scroll is not scattered while retrieving from the tool.

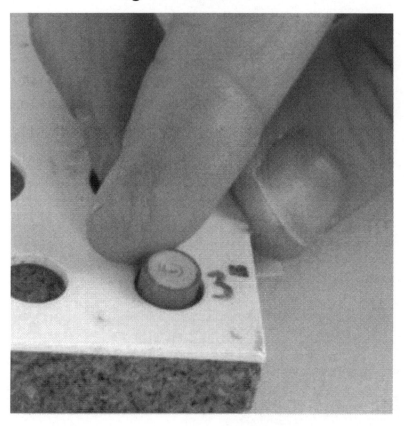

Gently, place the retrieved scroll in the holes of the template.

Be mindful of the hole size because the scroll will loosen when placed.

Repeat the process for all 5 scrolls.

4. Removing Scrolls from Template

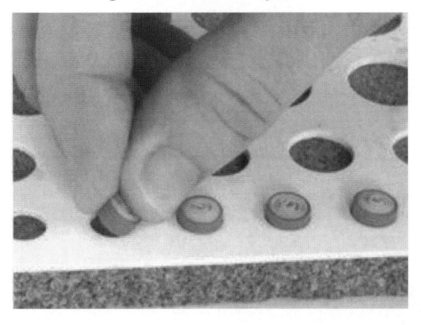

Carefully pick each of the 5 scrolls or whatever number of scrolls you're using.

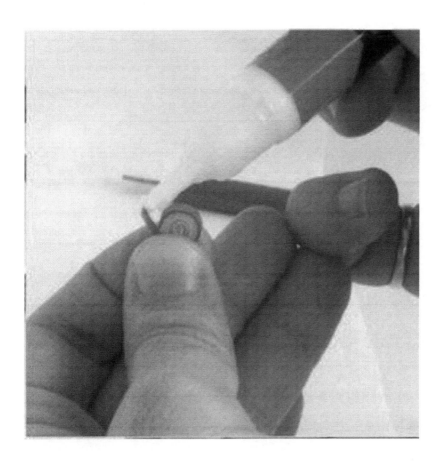

As you pick, glue the free edges of each scroll to lockdown the scroll against unfolding.

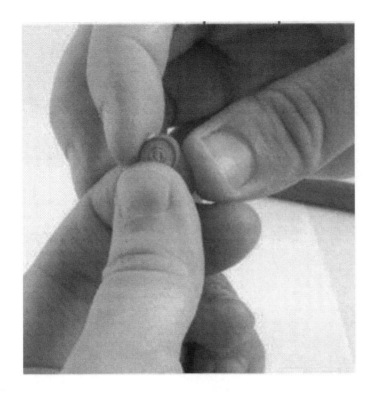

Allow scrolls to dry. Pick them out one after the other.

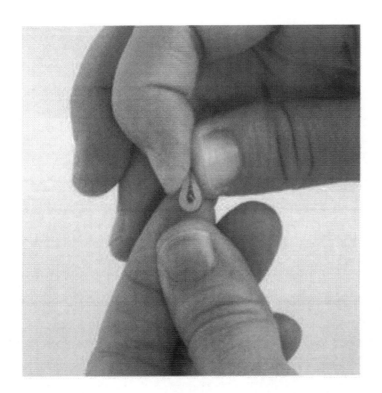

Hold the one edge of the scrolled quill down. Ensure that the held edge becomes somewhat pointy and gives a petal-like shape. Repeat this for all scrolls.

5. Gluing All 5 Petals

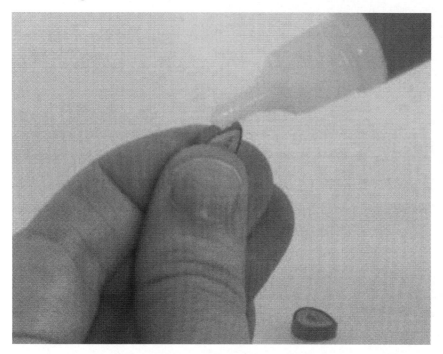

Apply glue using glue dispenser towards the pointy part of every petal-shaped quill.

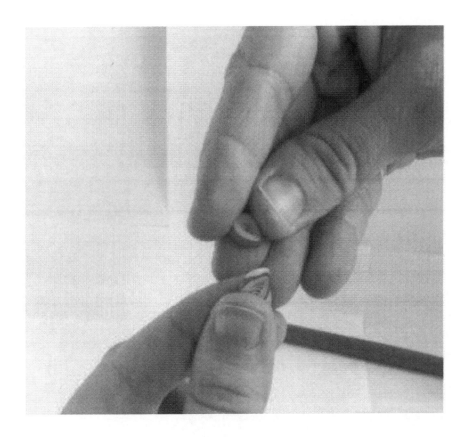

Place the glue parts together. Repeat the process until all five petals produce star-like shape.

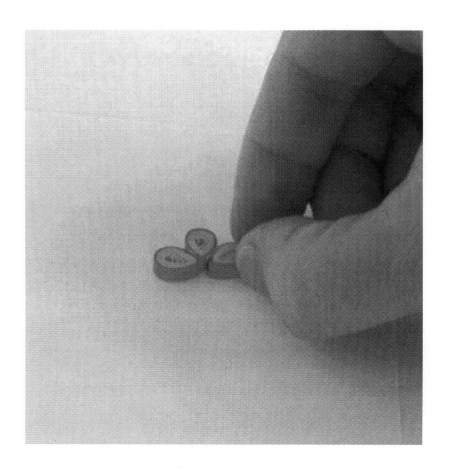

Ensure that the pointy edges of the petals face each other while making placement.

In the end, you should have something like this. Place on a board and allow to dry.

6. Arranging the Quill Daisy Earring with Pin

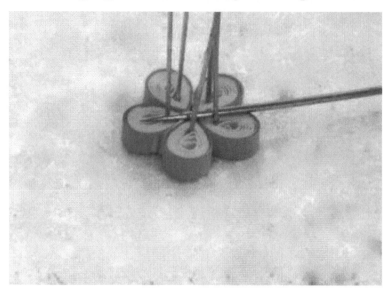

It is optional to give shape to the quilled daisy earring. While they are yet to dry, place pins on the areas with a bit of a distorted look. In my case, I do not have to place pins always. Sometimes, the quill comes out well arranged and sometimes I have to use pins to give it shape.

If you prefer quill earrings with a more opening, I recommend using 3" x 3" strips. Otherwise, use 6"x 3" strips for a tighter quilled earring.

Being that quills papers are delicate, you may want to apply sealants. I apply sealants on all my quilled earrings in order for them to resist water. If people using quilled earrings happen to find themselves out in the rain, they would have to worry less concerning their quilled earrings.

As simple and straightforward as this may seem, it is all you have to do to come up with a lovely quilled daisy earring. Simply follow the instructions and be attentive to the photos as well.

Would it be interesting if you choose to tweak this guide and maybe come up with something a bit different and unique? Of course, not. This is art and it is all about creativity. Besides, the making of paper quills evolves with time.

Paper Quilling Projects for beginners

How to Produce a Paper Quilled Monogram

Quilling is a papercraft that has been around for a long time is as yet famous today. Numerous crafters make quilled monograms to give as wedding endowments, or to use as divider stylistic layout. Folding paper strips into lovely masterpieces is simple enough in any event, for novices to accomplish amazing outcomes.

The contemporary visual creator and graphic designer, Yulia Brodskaya, began the quilled monogram fever. Her unique works propelled this new type of quilling that transforms typeface into quilled workmanship. Today, a significant number of her exceptionally valued masterpieces are claimed by superstars and private authorities.

You don't need to go through a ton of cash to begin with this art. All you need is paper, glue, and a round article, for example, a toothpick or a bamboo stick to twist the paper strips. In case you're nibbled by the quilling bug, you'll need to buy instruments, for example, a quilling pen, brush, and crimper. At that point, you can cause complicated flowers, to decorate cards, and even make adornments. With time, practice, and a smidgen of tolerance, you will before long become a paper craftsman.

Requirements Needed

- Gear/Tools
- Scissors
- Craft paper trimmer
- Tweezers
- Tacky glue, (for example, Mod Podge)
- 1 Paper plate or old plastic holder for stick
- Small paintbrush for sticking

Materials Needed

- Card stock or pre-cut quilling strips in wanted colors
- 1 sheet Thick card stock or board for the foundation
- 1 Shadowbox picture outline or frame

Procedures

1.Print Your Outline

Print your letter of decision, filled in with a light or dim foundation shade of your decision, onto the card stock foundation.

Voluntary Letter Method

On the off chance that you don't approach a printer, utilize this elective strategy for a letter:

1.Trace an enormous letter from a source, for example, a book or magazine, onto a piece of paper utilizing a pencil.

2.Use a light touch with the pencil, you would prefer not to see the pencil lines in your last task. It will be difficult to delete the lines after you assemble your casing.

3.Or, you can fill in the letter with a favored foundation shading that will look free from quilled pieces.

4.Use a ruler to make the straight lines.

5.If wanted, join the paper with the following onto a bit of card stock for the additional steadiness.

2.Cut the Strips to size

1.Choose card stock in colors you intend to join into your structure.

2.Use the paper shaper to cut paper takes from the card stock that measure one-quarter inch wide.

Pre-Cut Card Stock Strips

Rather than cutting strips, purchase bundles of pre-cut quilling paper on the web or at the art store.

3.Shape the Strips

When you choose what the structure of within your letter will be, it's an ideal opportunity to make shapes.

1.Take a paper strip and wind it around your toothpick or quilling device into the shape wanted, either moved firmly (for a reduced shape) or freely, contingent upon your inclination. Allude to the regular quilling shapes underneath.

2.Place a smidgen of glue onto the finish of the paper strip to hold the shape set up.

Sketch It Out

Prior to twisting your strips, take a good look at other quilled monograms for motivation and make a primer brisk simple picture for the format of your monogram.

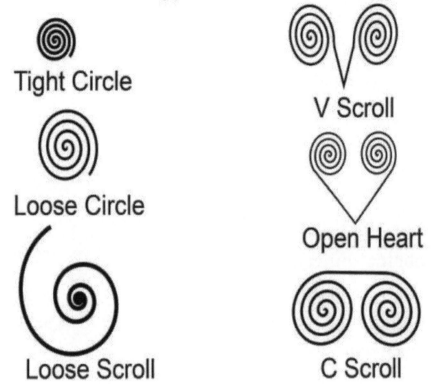

Six Common Types of Rolled Quilling Shapes

Tight Circle

Loose Circle

Loose Scroll

V Scroll

Open Heart

C Scroll

4.Use Paper Strips to Outline Your Letter

Utilize your favored technique to apply glue to the bits of paper that will shape the edge of your letter.

Glue: the lesser the quantity the better

A lot of glue can destroy your task, so be cautious. There are two different ways to apply glue to your straight segments of paper that structure the edge of your letter. (Use both of these strategies to put your formed and quilled pieces inside the letter outline, as well.)

1.Use a little brush and a light touch to apply glue to the edge of the paper.

2.Place the strips gently onto a paper plate with glue to softly cover the edge of a piece, at that point place on your framework.

5.Use Paper Strips to Frame the Outside of the Letter

1.Glue and spot your strips on the layout of your letter. Hold each strip down delicately until the glue is firm enough for the portion of paper to stand up all alone.

2.Make a fresh crease on a segment of paper and include a drop of glue each end and cover it on each corner. This little strip will make sure about the corners.

3.Glue and layer a quarter-inch strip as a stay anyplace else you have a joined portion of paper making the divider. The layering will make the edge more grounded.

4.Allow the mass of your quilled letter to dry altogether.

6.Begin Filling in Your Letter Frame

When you have constructed your external edge, fill in the internal parts of your monogram.

1.Follow your structure and glue your shapes and strips into place, utilizing your fingers and tweezers for restricted spaces.

2.Allow the completed piece to dry totally for a couple of hours.

7.Make Use of Your Tweezers

Tweezers are a quillers closest companion. They are one of the most significant apparatuses you will utilize on the grounds that it causes you pull paper states of all sizes into little spaces inside your monogram venture without upsetting the casing.

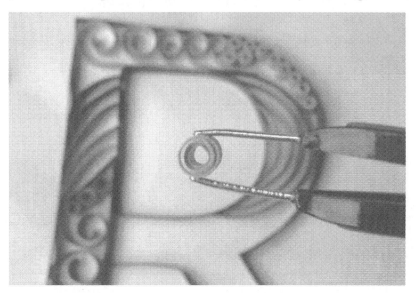

8.Framing the Completed Quilled Monogram

At the point when your piece is dry, place it in your shadowbox outline.

The Benefits of using a Shadowbox Frame

A standard picture outline with glass isn't sufficiently profound to house your quilled monogram. You will require a shadowbox that is at any rate an inch somewhere down so as to oblige the raised surface of the quilled venture.

Paper Quilling Flower Pendant

At the point when I was an adolescent and simply beginning to make my own gems, probably the greatest test I confronted was spending plan. I had a touch of spending space for the non-consumables and the bigger bundles: apparatuses that were reused from venture to extend, huge bundles of jumprings and earwires...

In any case, I battled with things like costly dots that were sold in amounts enormous enough for only one bundle. I likewise preferred to do things another way. Beaded gems is somewhat cool, yet it's... well, exhausting.

I mean it doesn't need to be (and you can see that inevitably I built up my own style with this wire wrapped gemstone wristband) however I despite everything love adding a measurement to my gems that is new, and utilizing remarkable materials.

In view of this, I have some good times shock seeking you on October eighth – stay tuned! In the event that you need to be advised of updates ensure you're a supporter (it's free)!

Presently, on to this paper quilling bloom pendant.

Paper quilling is a great side interest and the consumable supplies are so moderate! You can utilize bought quilling strips, or make you own, you need to keep up a consistency thus it very well may be dull. Quilling strips come in huge, reasonable bundles so it merits getting them premade.

Obviously, this paper adornments make isn't water safe so you'll need to get it far from water. You can seal it in the event that you'd like utilizing a sealer.

After you're finished making this paper quilling flower pendant, attempt it with different structures. Transform it into keyrings, make littler renditions as studs, and consolidate a couple quilled structures to frame an announcement neckband or wristband.

Requirements needed to make a paper quilling flower pendant:

- Quilling paper strips
- Glue
- quilling opened apparatus
- 4mm fake pearl dab (discretionary)
- Jump ring
- Finished chain or string
- Optional: extra globules to decorate chain

Procedures to making a paper quilling flower pendant:

1. Select a paper strip in your first shading, and utilize the opened quilling instrument to curl the strip.

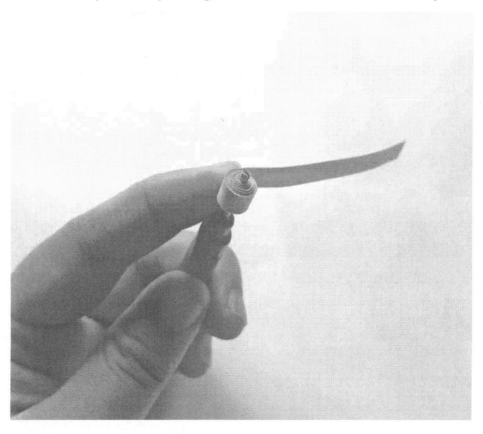

2. Subsequent to curling the whole strip cautiously remove it from the quilling instrument, holding the strip so it doesn't uncoil.Allow the curl to release up a piece.

3. Spot the inexactly looped strip on a level surface and paste a little dot in the focal point of the quilled circle (discretionary).

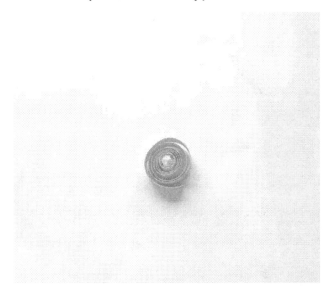

4. Fix the curl again by holding it between 2 fingers and pulling the open end. When the middle part has fixed, roll the remainder of the strip around it and apply stick at the tip to make sure about your curl. This will be the focal point of the paper quilling bloom.

5. Select a quilling strip in your subsequent shading and quill it utilizing the opened quilling instrument.

6. In the wake of quilling the strip cautiously remove it from the device.

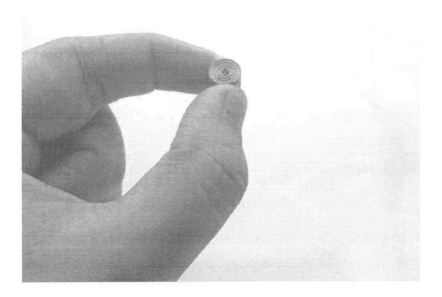

7. Permit the loop to slacken up a piece by setting it on a level surface.

8. Take the freely quilled example and squeeze one side to make a pointy edge. You presently have a tear shape.

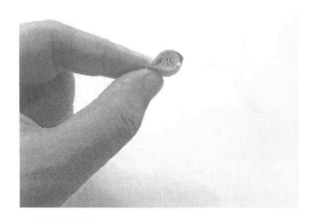

9. Presently squeeze the contrary side of the quilled strip to make another pointy edge. You presently have an eye shape.

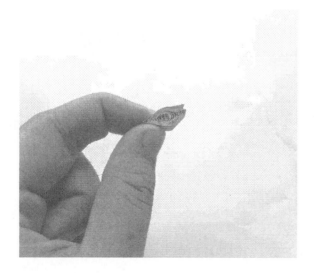

10. Replicate stages 6-10 to make 5 more eye shapes utilizing similar shaded strips for an aggregate of six. Make 3 more eye shapes in your third paper shading.

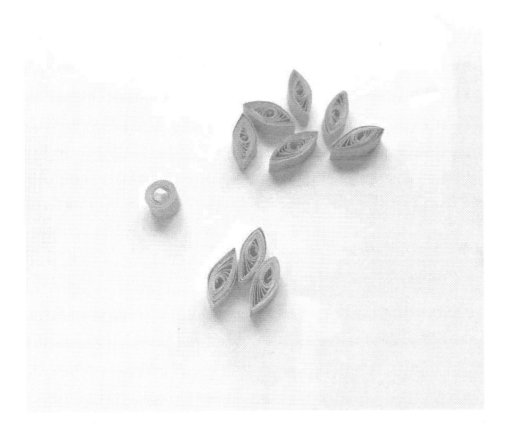

11. Take a bit of paper or plastic with a smooth surface (so you can undoubtedly eliminate stuck pieces). Spot the inside aspect of the bloom on your surface. Take your initial two eye shapes from your shading that you have six of and join them to the circle. Do this by sticking any of the pointy edges to the inside circle. Paste the adjusted aspect of the eye shapes to one another also, interfacing your petals.

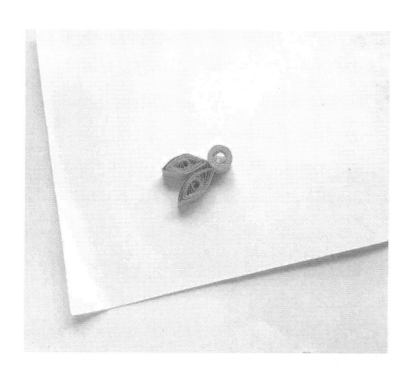

12. Presently take one from your second shade of eye-formed loops, and paste it a similar path to the inside and to the bordering petal.

13. Replicate your example until your paper quilling bloom shape is finished.

14. Make a tight curl with a moderately greater circle on the middle.

15. Append the curl to the bloom design between any two of your petals to fill in as a circle. On the off chance that you'd prefer to seal your plan, right now is an ideal opportunity to do as such. Ensure you leave the gap in the curl that you made in sync 15 open.

16. Connect a bounce ring however the circle of the loop to finish the pendant.

17. Connect your jump ring to a line or chain and wear with satisfaction! In the event that you'd prefer to include dots, you'll have to either complete your own chain, or eliminate the finishes that accompanied it and pick huge holed dots as accents.

Wear it and be glad for your paper quilling flower abilities!

Paper Quiling projects

Mother's Day Paper Quilling

Mothers are nature's blessings, and we should treat them as treasures. What do you have in mind for her? Money? New clothes? Maybe you should think of something else! How about paper quilling for a mother's day? Oh, yes! Such is a fantastic art for celebrating a lovely mother.

Moreover, you barely have a thing to worry about because this guide covers the basics of a proper mother's day paper quilling. Trust me; mum would be the most grateful and happiest in the world on her day.

Let's get started to avoid wishing her a belated mother's day.

Materials Required for Mother's Day Paper Quilling

- Knife
- Cocktail sticks
- PVA glue
- Ruler
- Scrap card
- A pair of scissors
- Thin quilling papers (gold, bright pink, pale pink, and navy blue)
- Spectroscope rainbow card (mint green, yellow, and lilac)
- Pencil
- Bulldog clips

How to Make Mother's Day Paper Quilling Step by Step

1. Create Heart-Shaped Drawing

In the absence of a heart-shaped tool, you may use freehand. However, you require a perfect heart-shaped design. Simply search for heart-shaped drawing online and print out a copy or two.

2. Rule Down 1.5cm

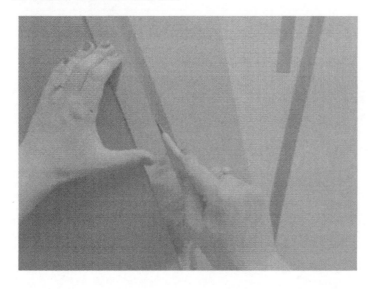

Use the ruler to rule 1.5cm down the opposite ends of the thin paper strip. Cut the paper strips from following the 1.5cm line using a knife. Repeat this process for all the required cards.

3. **The Bright Pink Quilling Paper**

Cut a strip of the bright pink quilling strip and gently apply glue (PVA) to either of the edges.

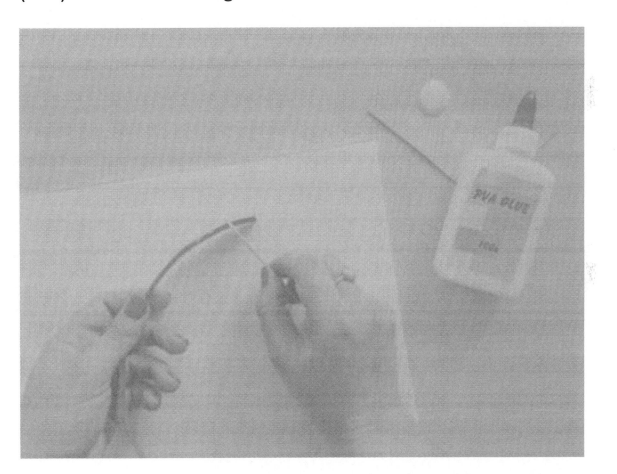

4. Forming Half Heart

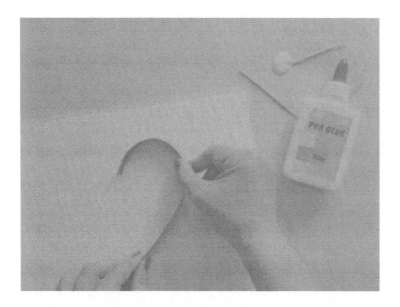

Place one of the bright pink paper strips on one side of the heart-shaped diagram as in the picture. Hold for at least 30 seconds for the glue to better clip the paper.

5. Glue the Final Edge

Pick up the second bright pink paper strip and place it on the diagram to ultimately form the heart-shape. Hold firmly for a few seconds for PVA glue to dry.

6. Make Triple Loop

You need three paper strip - pale pink, bright pink, and lilac paper strips. Take out 4cm of the pale pink strip, 6cm of the bright pink paper strip, and 8cm of the lilac paper strip.

a. Apply PVA glue to either or both ends of all strips.

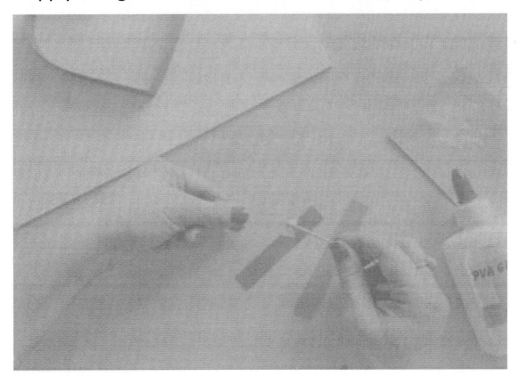

b. Pinch both ends of each paper strip together.

Encircle the first strip with another paper strip and then with a third, as in the picture.

c. Fit in the mini pegs to the pointy edges to hold the paper strips and allow some minutes for the glue to dry.

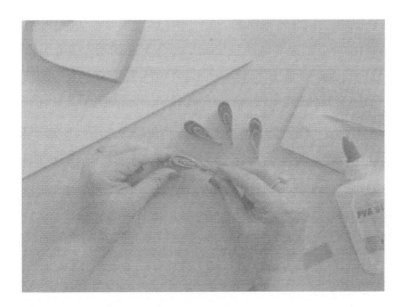

d. Attach the teardrop folds or triple loops to the heart-shaped quill as in the picture.

7. Make Coil Folds

a. You need lilac folds for making coil folds with regards to this tutorial. Place one end of the paper strip on the cocktail stick.

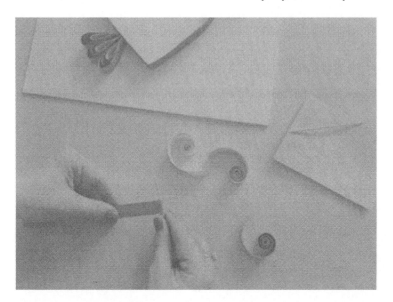

b. Curl the paper strip around the cocktail stick to make a coil fold. Hold the paper strip firmly on the cocktail stick to give it shape while you are curling.

c. Apply glue to hold down the strip.

d. Firmly press down one end of the coil fold to create a teardrop fold.

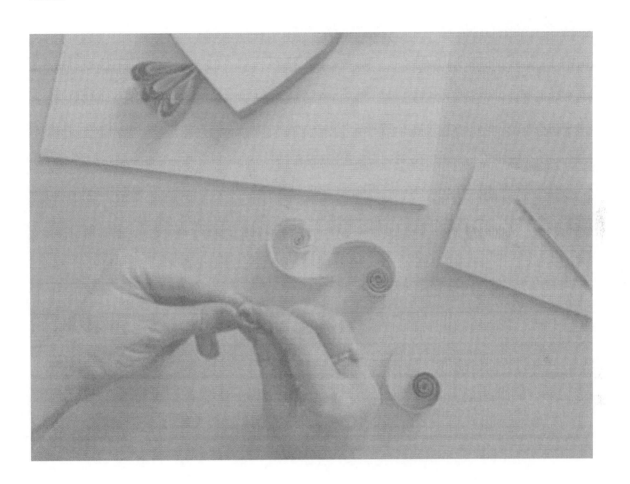

8. Make Green Loose coil Folds

Make three coil folds using the green strips and pinch both ends for marquis folds.

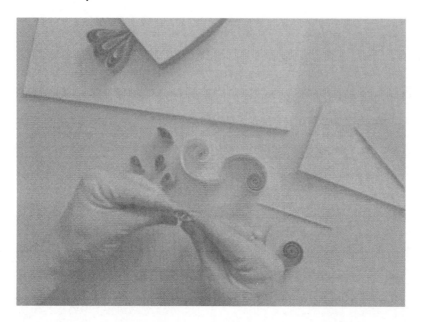

9. More Coil Folds

Make more coil folds from various colored paper strips and draw out the edges of some coil folds as in the picture.

10. Create Loops of Different Sizes

Use a pair of scissors to cut off the ends of some strips for the loop effect and place the paper strips as in the picture.

11. Create More Petals, Leaves, and Loops

Create as much petal, leave, and loop strips that fit the heart-shaped design.

Place them to see how it appears.

12. Apply Glue

Go ahead and apply the glue to hold down the strips.

13. It's Ready

Now, you have the much-adorned mother's day quilling set before you.

Quilling Paper Acorn

The splendor of artificially making natural products is realizable with the paper quilling art. Of course, quilling art suffers not a restriction to any design, expectation, or beauty; it is a magnificent art covering, to a broad extent, all spheres of nature's beauty.

The acorn, a fruit of the oak, is one of the million sweetness of nature that man can recreate with paper strips. How? The paper quill art? Is it possible to achieve such a difficult task of making paper strips into acorn(s)?

Sincerely, it is, and I will show how to make acorn quilling using acorn caps.

Materials Required for Quilling Paper Acorn

Acorn Caps

Get acorn caps from the plant in your home or check around your neighborhood. If there is no acorn fruit nearby, consider from Etsy. Clean up the acorn caps and allow them to dry if wet.

Glue

Must be able to glue paper strips on the acorn caps.

Slotted Quilling Tool

You may use a chewing stick as an alternative tool.

Paper Strips

Larger acorn caps require 48 inches of paper while you may need 36 inches' paper for smaller acorn caps.

How to Make Paper Quilled Snowflake Ornaments

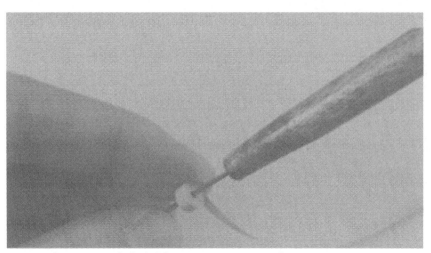

a. Make a coil fold by wrapping the paper strip around the slotted quilling tool.

b. Depending on the size of acorn caps, you may require additional paper strip. Simple, apply glue to the edge of the paper strip in the quilling tool and attach a new paper strip to proceed.

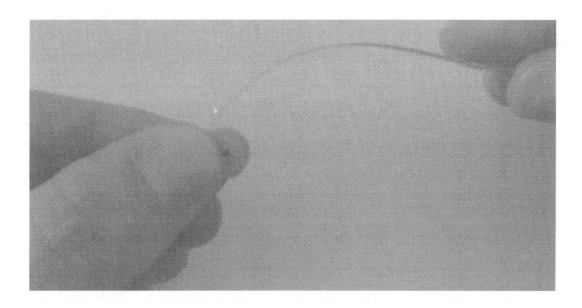

c. Keep folding for a coil fold until the fold becomes large enough to suit the size of the acorn cap.

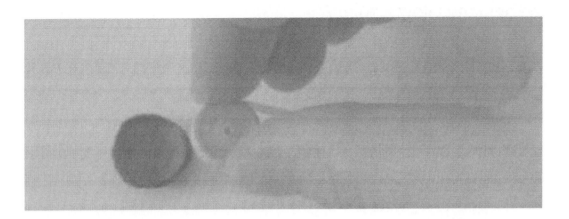

d. Measure the correctness of your fold with the acorn cap.

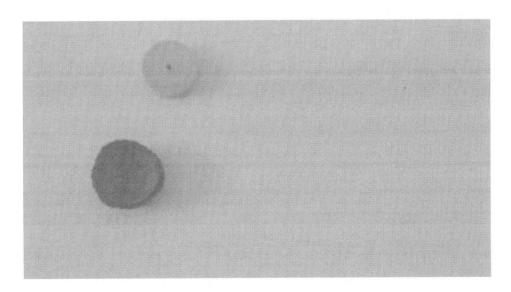

e. If it's satisfying, apply glue to the flapping edge of the strip, glue it together, and allow it to dry.

Making the Dome

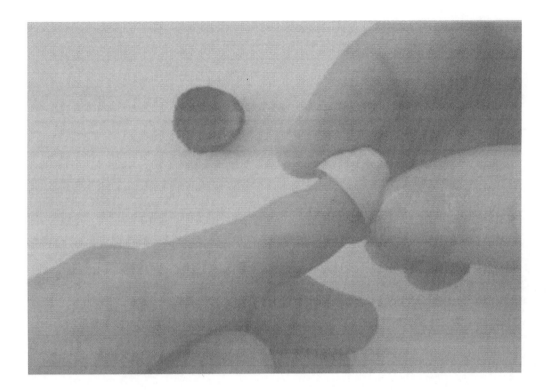

a. Once the glued coil fold is dry, you need to push your finger through the center of the coil fold to form a dome. You may use a pencil, pen, or any available cylinder-shaped item.

b. Apply glue inside the dome fold.

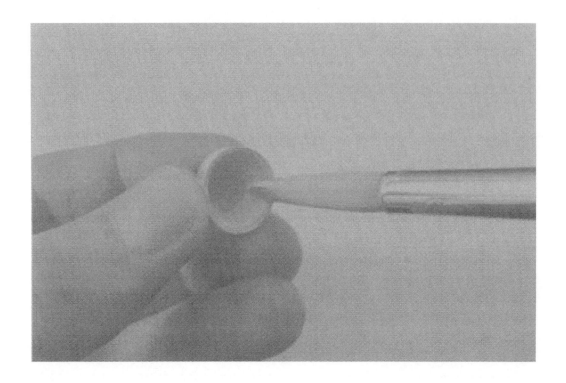

c. Disperse the glue within and allow it to dry. In a few seconds, your dome should take its shape.

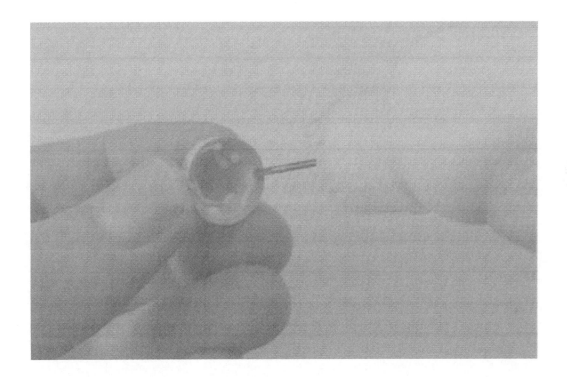

Attaching Acorn Cap in Dome

a. Pick up the dried dome folds and apply glue to the edges.

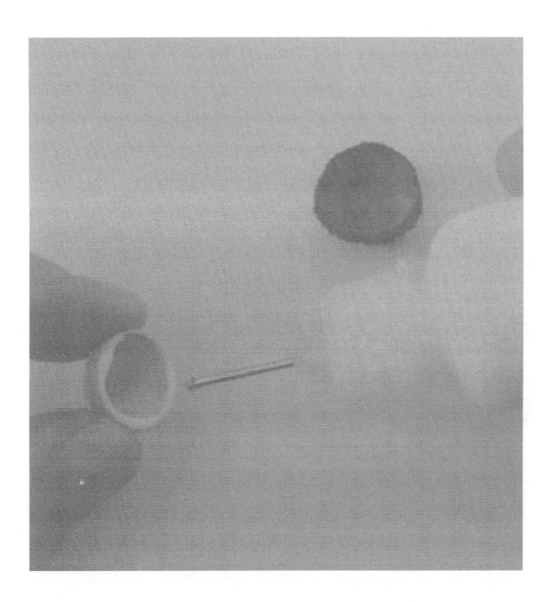

b. Pick and attach the acorn cap to the dome.

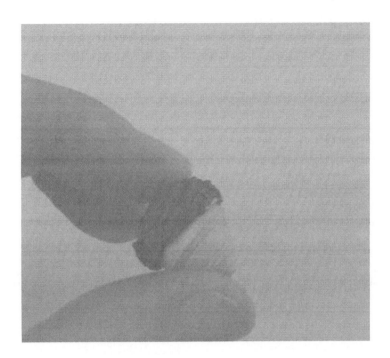

Your contagiously quilled paper acorns are ready! Check out the colorful quilled acorns below.

You may apply sealant on the dome folds to prevent water from causing a tear.

The Quilling Tutorial

Quilling is a contagious handicraft with no limitation. It is a form of art that provides room for the replication of anything in life. An artist, of course, is defined by his creativity, and creativity is what paper quilling is all about.

Paper quilling is an easy-to-do art; with just a few colorful paper strips and the mind, you would come up with something alluring. You could make the fashionable earrings, Christmas tree, mother's day quill, fruits of all kinds for decoration, etc.

Do you think it's tough to quill a design? I will disclose just how simple it is to achieve quilled designs.

Materials Required for Paper Quilling

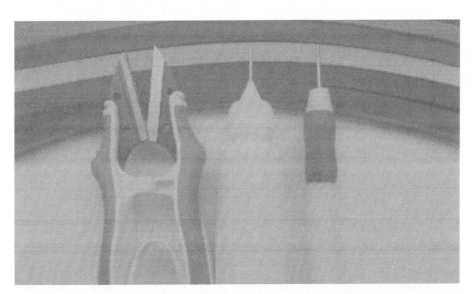

- A pair of scissors
- Slotted quilling tool
- Tweezers
- Paper strips

How to Make Coil Folds

a. Carefully, place one end of the paper strip near the edge of the slotted quilling tool. The paper strip should not be too close to the handle of the slotted quilling tool.

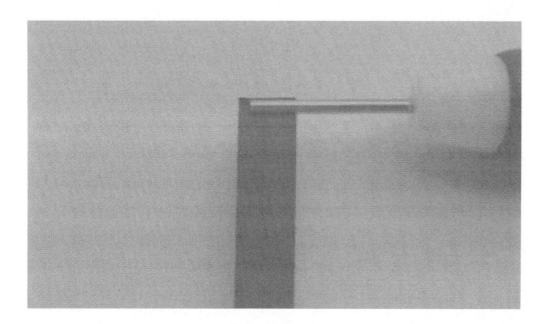

b. Roll the paper strip around the quilling tool until a little flap is left.

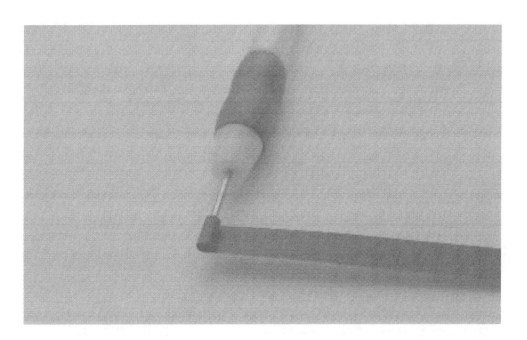

c. Apply glue to the tip of the remaining paper strip.

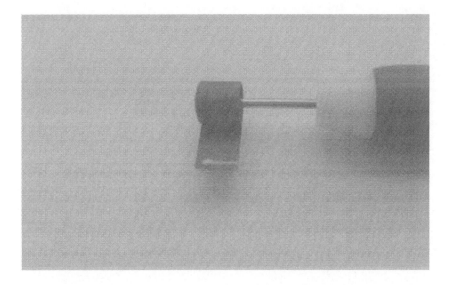

d. Clip the glued area to the body and allow it to dry.

The final size of the coil fold depends on the length and width of paper strips.

You can make use of various colors to achieve a colorful effect. Occasionally, you may use multiple but similar shades for a gradient effect. I am using varying shades of equal sizes.

Note: The paper color(s) matter for the design or what you are replicating.

How to Make Teardrop Folds

a. Create a coil fold. Withdraw the fold from the quilling tool and allow the fold to untangle.

b. Randomly pick and press one end of the fold, as in the picture.

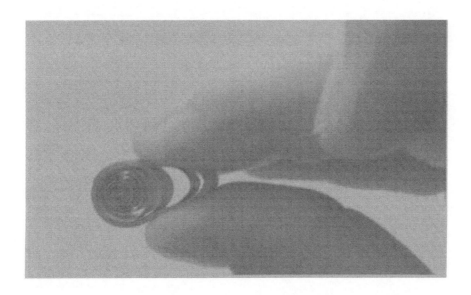

c. Below is how your teardrop fold should look.

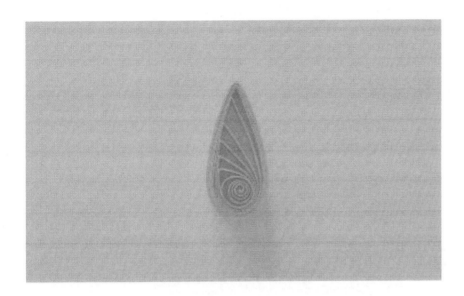

Variations of Teardrop Folds in Quilling

You can shape the teardrop folds into various beautiful shapes.

After forming your teardrop, curve the fold around your thumb and be careful not to compromise the central coils of the fold.

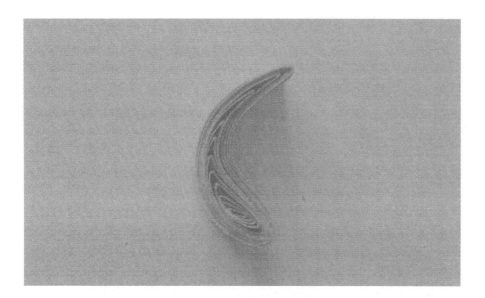

To make the shape more pronounced, wrap the teardrop around the slotted quilling tool or pencil.

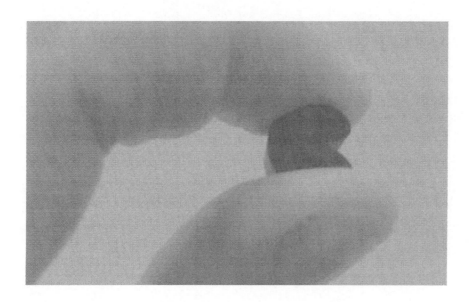

Withdraw the fold and press firmly with your fingers until it takes the desired shape.

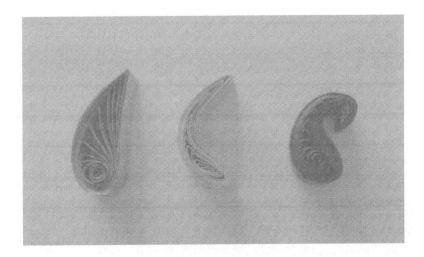

Use the idea to create as many variations of a teardrop as you wish.

How to Make the Marquis Fold

You can achieve a marquis fold design by pressing the opposite end a conventional teardrop fold. As in the picture below, you will realize an eye-shape fold, which, of course, is the marquis.

To make the fold more pronounced, press it down very tight.

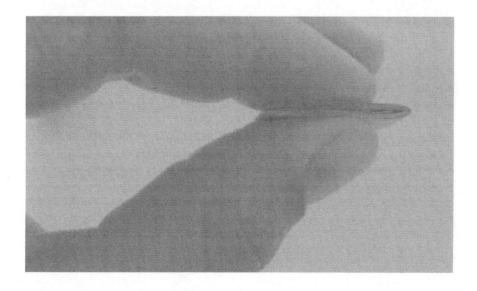

The more the pinching pressure you apply, the more pronounced the marquis fold will turn out.

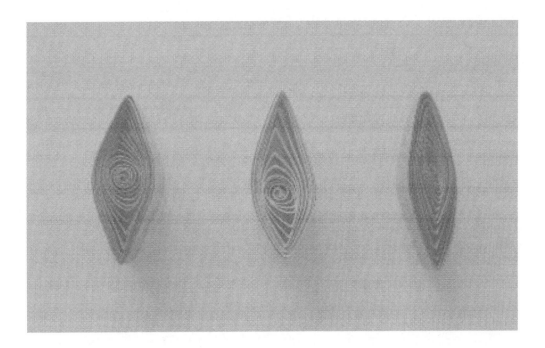

You could as well make a couple more designs out of the conventional marquis.

The designs I will create from the marquis include the following:

- Tulip
- Slug
- Diamond or Square

Making Tulip from Marquis

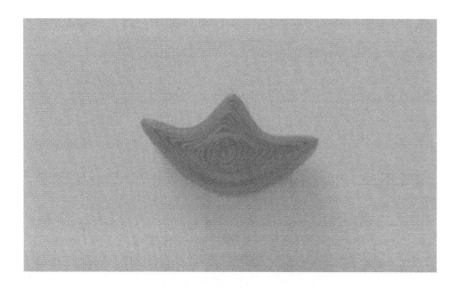

- Create a marquis shape.

- Pick one side of the marquis fold and pinch the middle outwards.

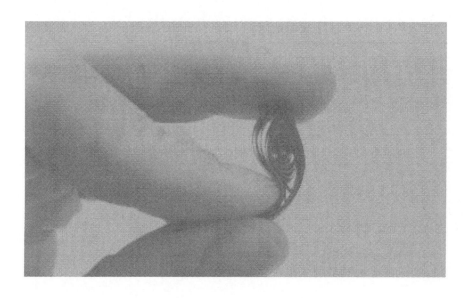

Making a Slug from Marquis Fold

- Create a marquis fold.

- As in the picture above, curl one end of the marquis fold around

- Repeat the curling process on the opposite end of the marquis to achieve the slug design.

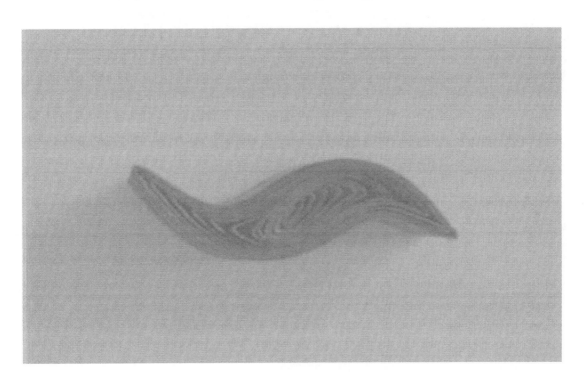

Making a Square or Diamond

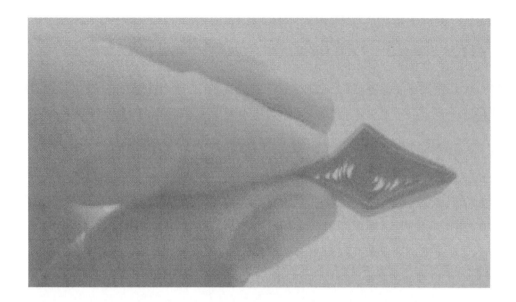

- Make a conventional marquis fold.

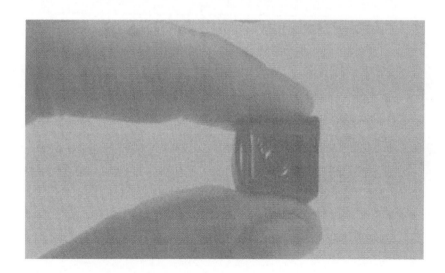

- Pinch out the opposite middles of the marquis fold.

For a perfect square, as in the picture above, use your finger to bend and pressurize the fold for a square shape. The harder the pressure, the more pronounced the resulting square-shaped fold.

Rectangle

- Rotate the marquis slightly lower than 90 degrees and pinch in between the center and the edge of the fold.

- Repeat the process for the opposite end, and you'll realize a rectangular fold.

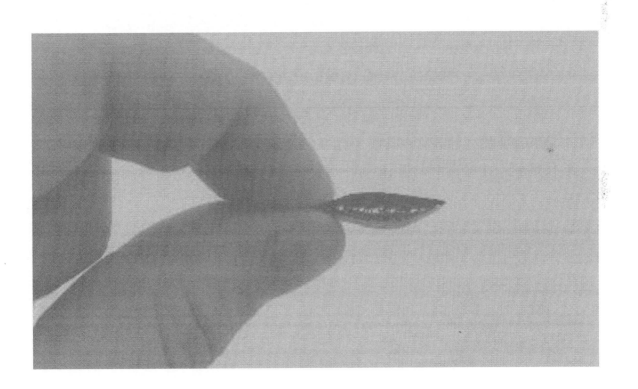

Use your fingers to shape the rectangular fold. Apply more pressure for a pronounced rectangular fold.

Variations of the Rectangular Fold

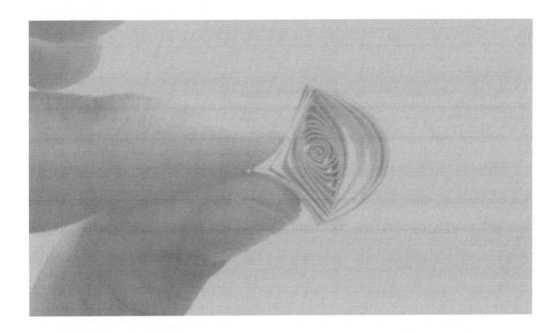

- Make a coil fold.

- Allow the fold to loosen, then pinch three ends - two opposite ends and one middle of the loose coil fold.

- Pinch four uneven points on the coil fold or the ends as in the picture above to achieve a quadrilateral shape.

The Semi-Circle Variation

Creating a semi-circle is quite easy. Simply, create a coil fold and allow the coil fold to loosen.

Firmly, pinch two ends of the coil fold, as in the picture above.

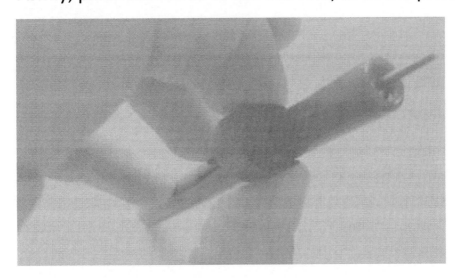

If you need a curvy semi-circle edge, press the plain edge against the handle of your quilling tool or any alternative tool.

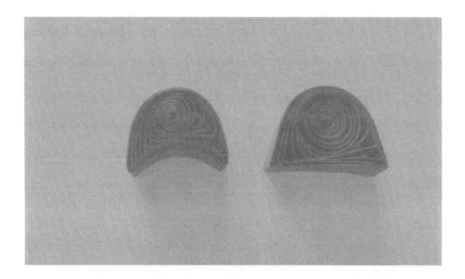

You should realize two fine semi-circles, as in the picture above.

The Triangle Fold

- First, create a teardrop fold.

- Pinch one end of the teardrop fold.

- Finally, pinch two more points just directly opposite the first edge.

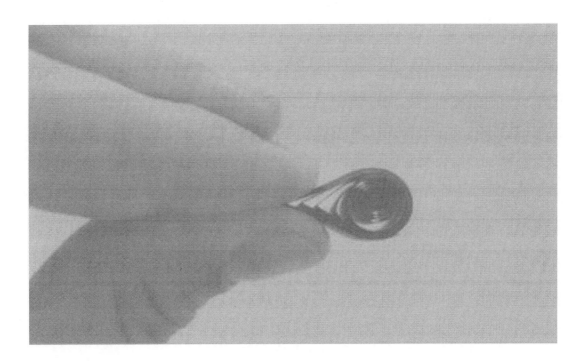

Arrow Fold

- Create a conventional teardrop fold.

- Use the quilling edge of the quilling tool to push in the opposite end of the pointy tip.

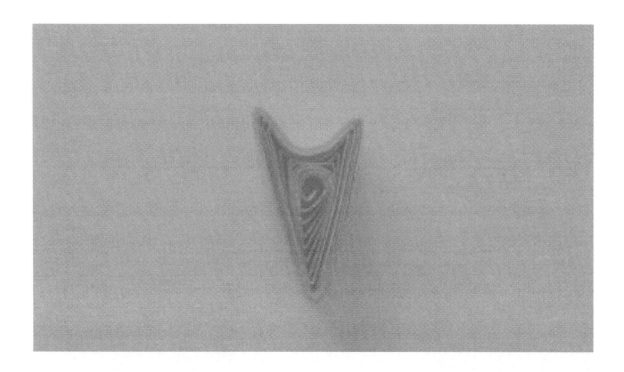

Now, apply as much pressure as possible to stabilize the fold.

Arrowhead Shape

Create a teardrop fold. As in the picture, pinch down three more points on the opposite end to form the arrowhead.

You can as well achieve the arrowhead shape using the marquise fold.

The Heart-Shaped Fold

Create a teardrop fold and use the edge of your quilling tool to push in the opposite end of the teardrop edge.

Use your fingers to pressurize around the heart-shaped fold for a sturdy fold.

The Pentagon and Start Shapes

- Create a coil fold.

- Release the fold to loosen.

- Pinch two ends of the coil fold to form a semi-circle shape.

- Release the fold to loosen (you may use your fingers to effect the release as in the picture above).

- Make a third pinch, as in the picture above.

- Make two more pinches as in the picture above to complete

- the pentagon shape effect.

The Star

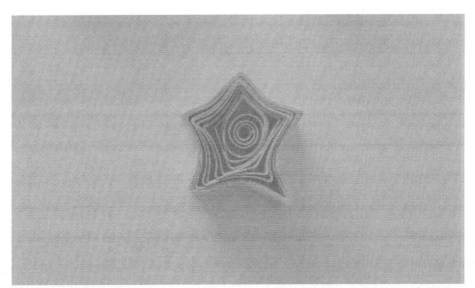

Create a pentagon shape and press the flat sides against a flat surface. Use a pencil or pen to shape the flat edges and your fingers to produce a better star shape by refining the edges.

The Holy Leaf

- Create a marquis fold.

- Insert the tweezers and grip a third of the outer part of the fold.

- While gripping with tweezers, turn the marquis fold to the pattern you desire.

Finally, retrieve the fold and pinch six ends, as in the picture above. The holly leaf is a complicated fold to make. However, it would not be so tricky if you master the art of making the preceding folds.

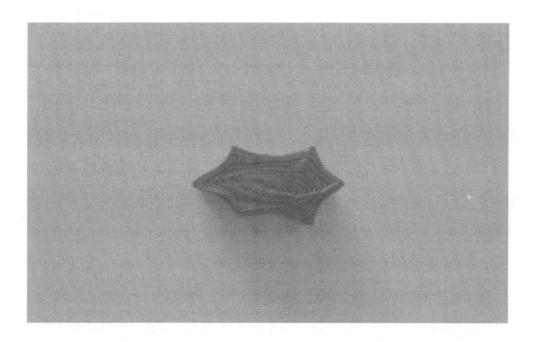

More Paper Quiling projects

How to Make Paper Quilled Flower Materials

Below are the basic materials required to do paper quilled flower on your own. Refer to the photo if you can't identify of the materials.

- 5 paper strips (6 inches long)
- Another 5 paper strips (3 inches long)
- Slotted quilling tool
- Paper glue
- Corkboard
- Pins
- A circle-sizing tool (It may be a board as well with hole)

The strips may be any preferred color as long as it suits the occasion.

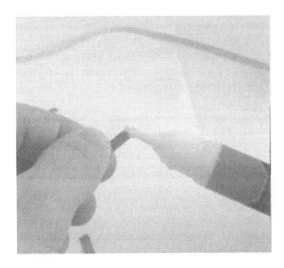

1. Gluing Both Strips

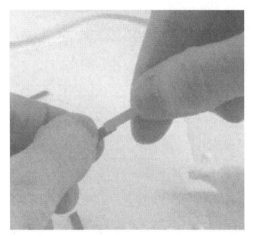

Apply paper glue at the preferred edges of each strip (3" and 6").

Bring the edges of each strip where you applied glue. Note, the strips you are gluing together must not be the same inches i.e. only 3" strips must be paired with 6" strips.

2. Rolling the Quilling Paper

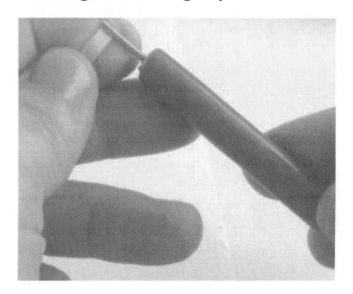

Pick up the slotted quilling tool. Place one edge of the glued strips at the tip of the tool.

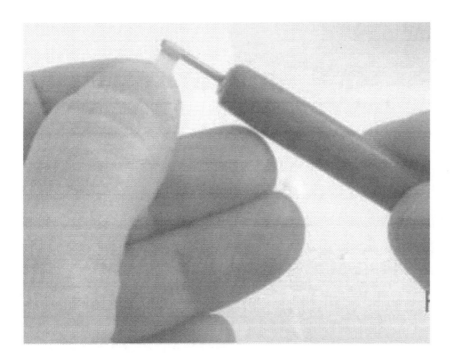

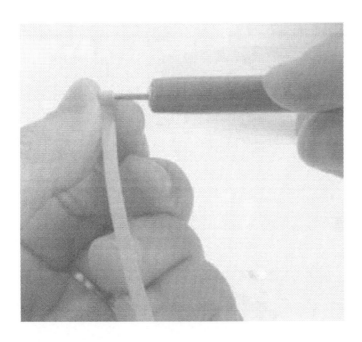

Start turning the quilling tool.

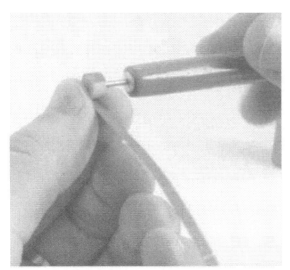

Ensure that you hold firm but not tight.

Go gently and keep rolling until the entire length of the strip is consumed.

3. Remove the Quilling Tool

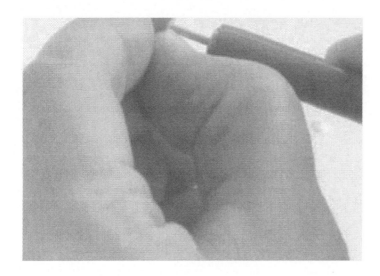

Add a light pressure using your forehand and thumb to press the strip to the quilling tool.

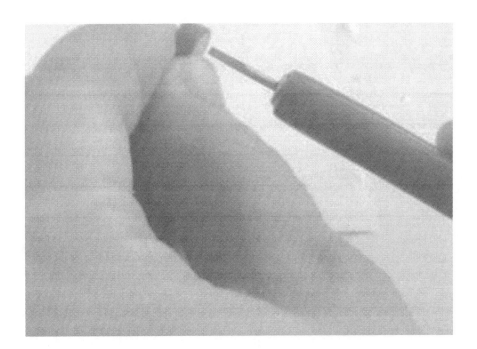

Carefully remove the scrolled paper from the quilling tool or whatever you're using. Ensure that the scroll is not scattered while retrieving from the tool.

Gently, place the retrieved scroll in the holes of the template. Be mindful of the hole size because the scroll will loosen when placed.

Repeat the process for all 5 scrolls.

4. Removing Scrolls from Template

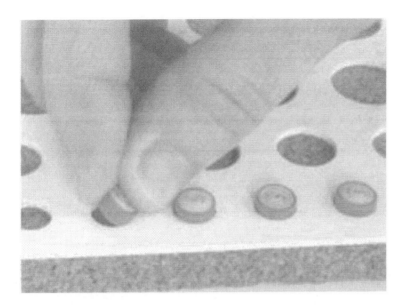

Carefully pick each of the 5 scrolls or whatever number of scrolls you're using.

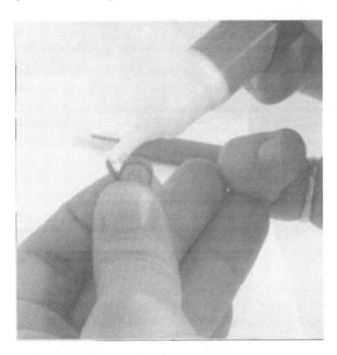

As you pick, glue the free edges of each scroll to lockdown the scroll against unfolding.

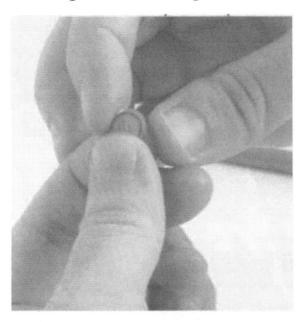

Allow scrolls to dry. Pick them out one after the other.

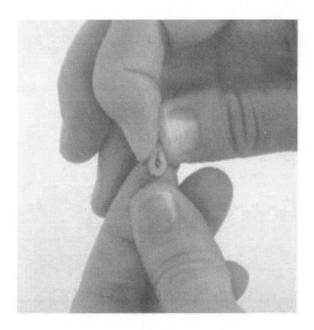

Hold the one edge of the scrolled quill down. Ensure that the held edge becomes somewhat pointy and gives a petal-like shape. Repeat this for all scrolls.

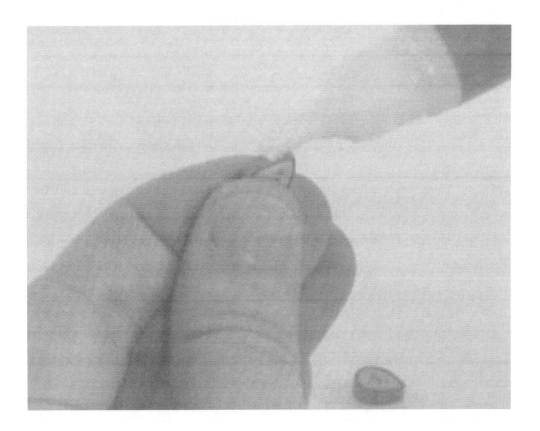

5. Gluing All 5 Petals

Apply glue using glue dispenser towards the pointy part of every petal-shaped quill.

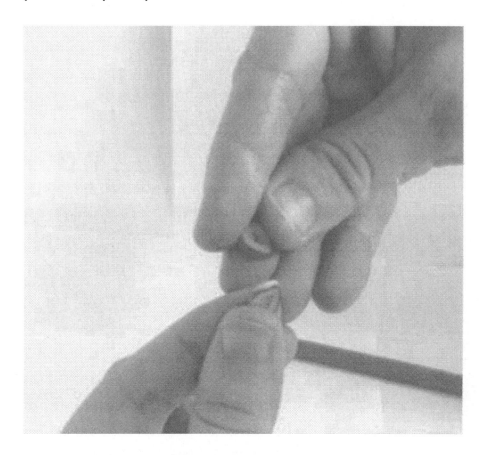

Place the glue parts together. Repeat the process until all five petals produce star-like shape.

Ensure that the pointy edges of the petals face each other while making placement.

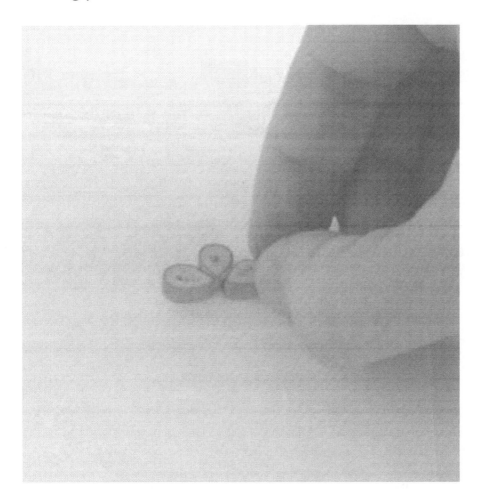

In the end, you should have something like this. Place on a board and allow to dry.

6. Arranging the Quill Daisy Earring with Pin

It is optional to give shape to the quilled daisy earring. While they are yet to dry, place pins on the areas with a bit of a distorted look. In my case, I do not have to place pins always. Sometimes, the quill comes out well arranged and sometimes I have to use pins to give it shape.

If you prefer quill earrings with a more opening, I recommend using 3" x 3" strips. Otherwise, use 6"x 3" strips for a tighter quilled earring.

Being that quills papers are delicate, you may want to apply sealants. I apply sealants on all my quilled earrings in order for them to resist water. If people using quilled earrings happen to find themselves out in the rain, they would have to worry less concerning their quilled earrings.

As simple and straightforward as this may seem, it is all you have to do to come up with a lovely quilled daisy earring. Simply follow the instructions and be attentive to the photos as well.

Would it be interesting if you choose to tweak this guide and maybe come up with something a bit different and unique? Of course, not. This is art and it is all about creativity. Besides, the making of paper quills evolves with time.

Paper Quilled Snowflake Patterns

It costs a few minutes to make and hold snow in your palm. That sounds great, considering that you would love to play around with snow even in summer!

The children and adults alike love to warble in snow. The elders may not be virile enough to jump around snow, which is why hand-crafted snow folds are preferable.

Interestingly, you require no much vigor or energy to build snow. Yes, you read that right, and you'll learn just how possible and easy.

Within a few minutes, this simple guide will reconcile your curiosity and further make you a unique paper quill artist.

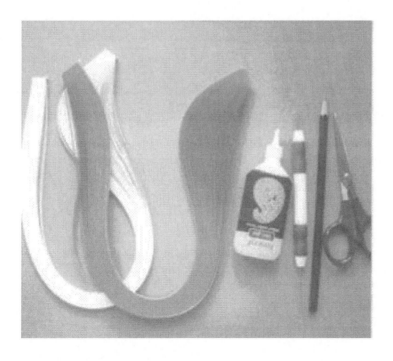

Materials Required for Paper Quilled Snowflake

- A pair of Scissors
- Quilling paper strips (blue and white)
- Pencil
- Quilling Glue
- Glue dispenser
- Quilling pins
- Geometric compass
- Quilling tool
-

Quilled Snowflake Folds

Here are the number of folds and types of folds needed with regards to the snowflake quilling done in this guide.

- 18 blue quarter-length tight coils
- 6 white length tight coils (54cm)
- 6 white length marquis (54cm)
- 6 blue length teardrops (54cm)
- 6 blue half-length tight coils
- 6 white quarter-length marquis
- 1 white half-length tight coils

How to Make Paper Quilled Snowflake Ornaments

1. Paper Length/Width: 54cm x 5mm

Paper strips should be 54cm long and 5mm wide. Use a ruler to measure the length for perfection carefully.

2. Create a Circle on the White Paper

Insert the pencil and carefully stretch the compass about 5cm to 6cm wide. Place the compass at the center of the white sheet and carefully rule a perfect circle. Finally, use the pencil to divide the circle into six visible equal parts.

3. Drawing the Floral

It may be difficult for a beginner to draw the floral. However, you can achieve the floral effect by doing the following:

- Draw a half-cm circle at the center of the larger circle.

- Draw six small circles around the small circle.

- As in the picture above, draw six more oval-like shapes.

- Make another six longer oval-like shapes round the six small circles.

- At the tip of the shorter oval-like shapes, create one large and one small circle as in the picture.

- Create four more circles at the tip of the six longer oval-like shapes, as in the picture.

4. Crafting the Various Folds

In this guide, I am using three different paper folds including marquis, coil, and teardrop folds.

Crafting the Marquis Folds

The marquis fold is an eye-shaped fold that involves pressurizing both ends of the folded quilling paper for the marquis effect.

 Fold all 6 of the 54cm length white marquis around the quilling tool or any available tool. Withdraw the quilling tool and pad each of the six folds gently with your fingers.

Press both ends of each white 54cm folds gently until you achieve an eye-shape. Release the pressure for the fold to loosen, pick and apply glue to the edge of the fold.

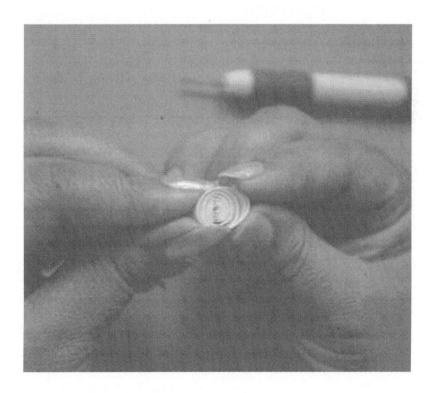

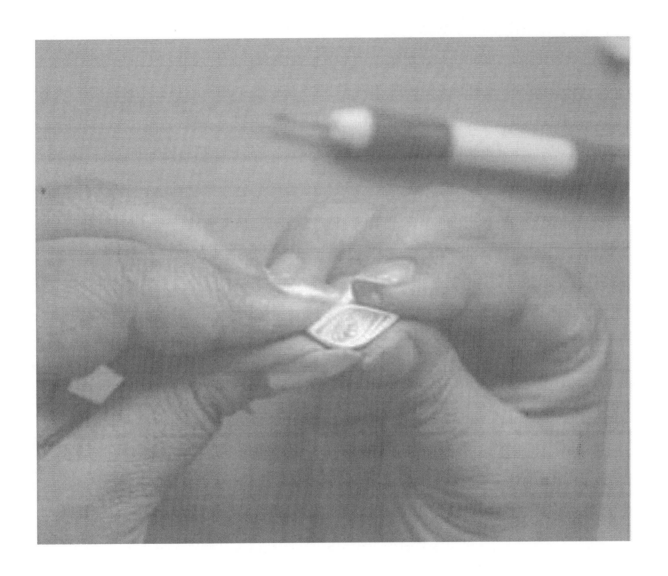

Crafting the Coil Folds

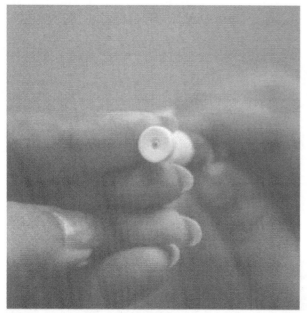

Wrap a 54cm fold around the quilling tool.

Retrieve the quilling tool and glue the flapping edge of the fold.

Crafting the Teardrop Folds

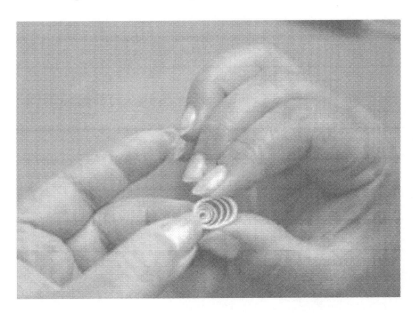

Wrap a new fold around the quilling tool. Retrieve the quilling tool and release the fold to loosen.

Firmly hold one end of the fold to create a tip-like design as in the picture and apply it to the flapping edge.

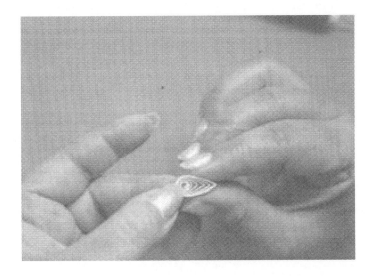

5. Applying Folds to the Drawing

Endeavor to place the marquis, teardrop, and coil folds in the corresponding areas of the circle. Make sure they each match the diagram, or it may distort the design.

Place each fold on the corresponding shape on the circle. Begin with the central coil fold, followed by the surrounding circular coil folds.

Place all six marquis folds, followed by all six teardrop folds in their corresponding positions. Repeat the process for the coil folds by placing a coil fold on each of the teardrop folds.

Place the remaining coil folds on the corresponding positions surround the teardrop and marquis folds. Place the half-done snowflake paper quill on a flat surface and apply glue to each fold carefully. Allow the glue to dry, and your lovely snowflake is ready.

You may optionally coat with a sealant to protect against water. Send your paper quills to loved ones as winter or summer gifts. During winter, make as much snowflake quills as possible and decorate your surrounding with them.

Guess what? Your crafted snowflake paper quilling can stay for as long as you desire; so far, you handle with care and coat with sealant.

Paper Quilled Teardrop Vase

Your vase is beautiful, but you can enhance the beauty by making it into something alluring with paper quilling art. It is quite simple, and a matter of quilling folds into teardrops using at least four different colors if you desire a gradient effect.

This guide discloses a simplistic way of fashioning a vase with the paper quilling art. In a matter of minutes, your first ever-alluring quilled teardrop vase should be ready.

Materials Required for Paper Quilled Snowflake

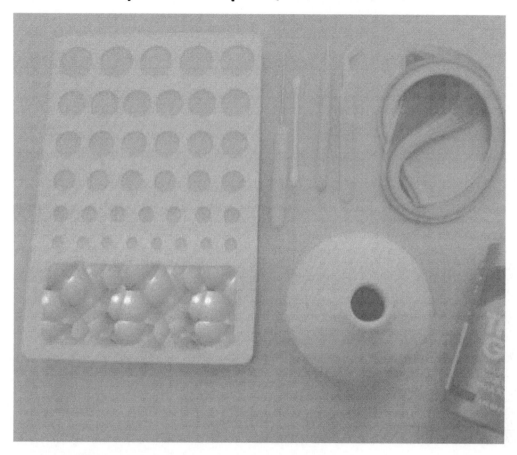

Paper Strips

In this guide, I am using a small set of paper strips with gradient colors. You may use one color, but you won't achieve the gradient effect.

Vase

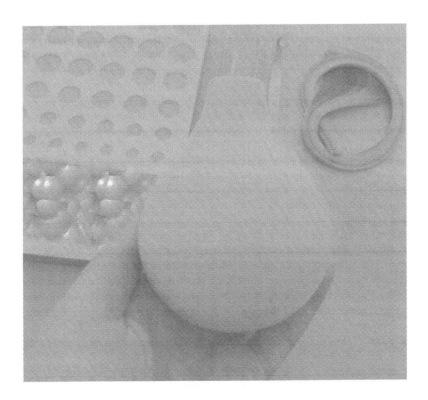

The vase must not be too curvy. It will be challenging to place the teardrop folds on an overly curvy vase. Get something smooth, and that would support the placement of folds.

Paper Glue

The glue must be such that it can glue the quilled paper on ceramic.

Quilling Needle

A cocktail stick wouldn't be a bad idea, but a quilling needle is ideal.

Quilling Board

The quilling board comes in various sizes. Depending on the size you would prefer, get a quilling board for the paper quill. Alternatively, you may use create circles on a plain sheet and use it to determine the sizes of each of the folds you make.

Slotted Quilling Tool

Necessary to make folds. You can alternatively use a chewing stick.

How to Make Paper Quilled Teardrop Vase

1. Create Coil Folds

Pick and place each quilling paper on the quilling tool. Endeavor to make the placement at the tip of the quilling tool to be able to control the spiral shape.

Fold each coil around the quilling tool carefully.

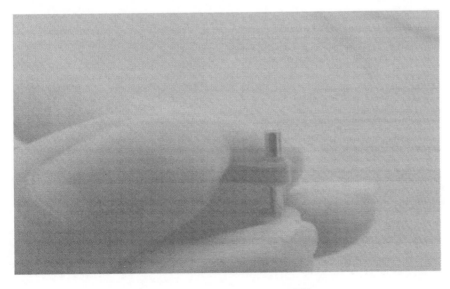

When done, hold the paper firmly but not too tight to give it excellent shape.

Withdraw the coil folds from the quilling tool and place it carefully in the quilling board and allow for loosening. In the absence of a quilling board, make sure that each fold fits the size of the circle you created on a plain sheet.

Repeat this process for all the quilling papers.

2. Make the Teardrop Effect

Withdraw each of the coil folds from the quilling board.

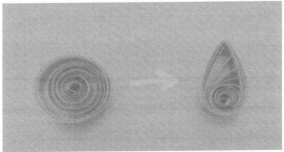

Place you two fingers at one end of the coil fold.

Gently, press that end to form a tip.

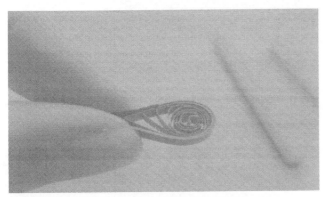

Hold it tight with added pressure.

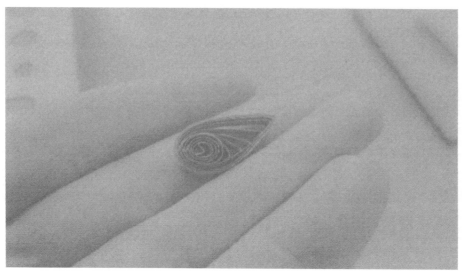

You should now have a well-made teardrop fold.

Place the teardrop fold on the quilling board and repeat the process for every paper.

3. Decorate the Vase with the Teardrop Folds

Pick up, clean your vase, and arrange the teardrop folds according to their colors.

Beginning from the bottom of the vase, apply paper glue to the teardrop folds and glue each fold to the vase.

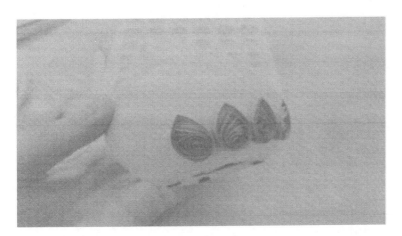

Continue the gluing process and fill up the bottom of the vase. A darker fold color is preferable if you're beginning from the bottom of the vase.

Repeat the gluing process for the second row of the vase. This time, the color of the fold should be lighter than the color of the fold at the bottom for the gradient effect.

Again, attach each teardrop fold to the vase in the third row. Endeavor to use a color different from that of the second row, as in the picture above.

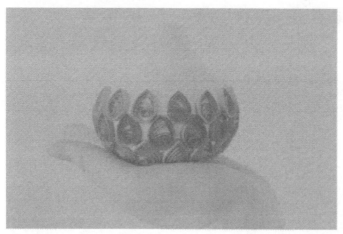

Finally, use a lighter color for the fourth row to complete the gradient effect.

You now have a lovely quilled teardrop vase

Note: Depending on the size of your vase, you may attach teardrop folds for more than four rows. If you intend covering the entire vase with the teardrop drops, endeavor to resize the teardrop folds when you reach the curvy part of the vase. Retaining the longer teardrops will result in a distorted quilling in that area.

Now that you have an elegantly crafted quilled teardrop vase, you may send it across to loved ones or share your knowledge with friends.

Conclusion

Quilling is easy to learn compared to other crafts, and with a lot of resources available today, it can be learned by almost anyone interested. I've given out basic quilling techniques, and I suggest that you also visit YouTube and join a number of life classes to improve your skills.

Quilling is becoming more popular, and a lot of people are starting to enjoy the craft. It is sometimes used for Christmas, greeting cards, scrapbooks, wedding invitations, birth announcements, and boxes. Quilling can be found in many art galleries in the United States and Europe, and it is an art practiced around the world.

Everyone loves a good comeback story, and the craft world is no exception. Quilling first came on the scene in the 16th century and enjoyed a surge of popularity by children and adults alike in the 1970s and '80s. Paper strips were rolled into incredibly realistic flowers and charming adornments for greeting cards. Like so many crafts of the past, however, quilling mostly faded away. Thankfully, a few dedicated quillers continued to share their skills and now a new wave of quillers are bringing a fresh set of eyes (and fingers) to what is often thought of as a dated craft.

Quilled Jewelleries

One place quilling is finding a new life is in jewellery or wearable art. Once you conquer the basic skills, it is quite easy and enjoyable to make. Relatively new tools allow quillers to create a variety of new shapes and endless possibilities for putting shapes together. Additionally, quilled jewellery has the benefit of being a bit more of an "instant gratification" type of project since you can easily complete many designs in just a couple of hours.

Quilled Art

On the opposite side of instant gratification comes the intensely time-consuming quilled paper art. Commissioned works are seen in many of today's most popular magazines, and paper artists are using paper quilling as their medium of choice to create spectacular works of art.

On-edge quilling or quillography are two terms most often used when referring to this type of quilling. Using card stock or multiple strips of quilling paper glued together, the paper is manipulated into the shape desired and then glued down on one side to give the illusion of 3-D illustration.

Quilled mosaics

Quilled mosaics are another example of using traditional quilling in a modern way. Using a wider quilling paper than the norm, mosaic artists create in a way that can only be described

as painting with paper. Using the basic quilled shapes, quillers manipulate and piece them together in a mosaic fashion. This work is incredibly time consuming,

But the payoff is big.

3-D Quilling

Another way that quilling is changing this time around: It's going upward and off the page. No longer must quilling be glued down and stationary, a tradition that really limits what can be accomplished. Newer quilling paper brands offer wider and heavier weighted paper than was typically available in the past, thus allowing quillers to create paper sculpture, useable and novelty items that would have been difficult to accomplish 30 years ago.

The ability to create whatever is in your mind's eye has so many advantages. Creativity can really shine in endless ways. The little fish television set was eventually made into an ornament, and it would also make an excellent keychain or zipper pull for your favorite wee one.

Embellishment quilling

Not to be left behind, quilling is still an excellent way to embellish cards, scrapbooks, invitations, gift tags, picture frames and much more. These types of projects have been enjoyed by quillers since the start, but the availability of more colour options and modern

Quilling tools have breathed new life into an old standard. Combining classic technique, 3-D quilling and a sense of artistry, quillers are taking paper crafting to a whole new level.

Whatever your skill level, wherever your interest lies, quilling has a little something for everyone. Hopefully these bright and modern paper quilling ideas will spark a new interest for those of you who have yet to give the craft a try and ignite a spark of creativity a new for those who have.

There are other corresponding books that focus on projects that can be developed by quilling. If you have children, you can introduce this craft to them as it teaches fine motor skills and a great craft to improve hand-eye coordination.

Practice makes it perfect, they say, isn't it? So, once you master the basic techniques of paper quilling, it'll take hours of creative fun to produce beautiful quilling designs and patterns.

Cheers. Cheers.